LEGENDS OF
AUTUMN

DENNY BOYD & BRIAN SCRIVENER

LEGENDS OF
AUTUMN
The Glory Years of Canadian Football

GREYSTONE BOOKS

Douglas & McIntyre
VANCOUVER/TORONTO

To Julianna, Mark and Claudia, and to my mother, the original fan   BAS

To By Bailey—88 forever   DB

Greystone Books
A division of Douglas & McIntyre Ltd.
1615 Venables Street
Vancouver, British Columbia
V5L 2H1

CANADIAN CATALOGUING IN PUBLICATION DATA

Boyd, Denny, 1930–
  Legends of autumn

  ISBN 1-55054-591-7

  1. Canadian Football League—History.   2. Canadian football—History.
I. Scrivener, Brian.   II. Title.
GV948.B69 1997   796.335´64   C97-910391-6

Editing by Barbara Pulling
Jacket and text design by Peter Cocking
Jacket photograph: Montreal Alouettes Red O'Quinn and Hal Patterson during the 1956 Grey Cup
  game, courtesy Canadian Football Hall of Fame
Typeset by Val Speidel
Printed and bound in Canada by Friesens
Printed on acid-free paper ∞

Every attempt has been made to trace accurate ownership of copyrighted visual material in this book. Errors will be corrected in subsequent editions, provided that notification is sent to the publisher.

The publisher gratefully acknowledges the support of the Canada Council for the Arts and of the British Columbia Ministry of Tourism, Small Business and Culture.

Contents

INTRODUCTION

There was a time, not so long and yet forever ago, when football filled the hearts of Canadians. That seems improbable from today's vantage point, when those who care about the game apologize for it, and those who don't consider it irrelevant. But then, in the brief span each year between first harvest and first snowfall, the game of football focussed the attention of the nation. What went on between the sidelines mattered, as a statement of regional rivalry as much as a celebration of athletic excellence. The game's greats were role models for a generation of youth, their portraits clipped from *Weekend Magazine* or *Star Weekly* and thumbtacked to a million bedroom walls.

There was a dynamic element afoot in Canadian football that resonated with the vigour of Canada itself. For both, the postwar quarter-century was a time of great vitality, growth and change. Canada's population grew by more than half between war's end and 1970, and the world its citizens knew changed beyond recognition.

Think about it. It was an era that began in the twilight of William Lyon Mackenzie King's third term and ended in the reign of Pierre Elliott Trudeau. In 1946, John Diefenbaker could say, "British methods have worked through the ages, and British methods will work today," with little fear of contradiction. By the end of the 1960s, Canada had expunged all trace of empire from its new flag and celebrated a century of nationhood with a year-long party.

The era began in an atmosphere of willful innocence, as a nation traumatized by two decades of Depression and war sought solace in the fiction of two-kid, two-car prosperity. At its end, the imposition of the War Measures Act in response to FLQ bombings and kidnappings exploded the myth that our nation was one big happy family.

When it began, television broadcasting had yet to commence. By the time it ended, we had watched a man walk on the moon. When it began, it was perfectly natural for a player to be described as "a fine Negro running back" in the sports pages. By the time it ended, American sprinters John Carlos and Tommie Smith had raised their fists in a Black Power salute on the podium at the Mexico Olympics and Martin Luther King lay dead by an assassin's hand.

Along the way, Canadians gained a Bill of Rights, Medicare, the Official Languages Act, all strong threads in the social fabric that we take for granted today. Newfoundland became a province. The St. Lawrence Seaway opened. The last Canadian was executed for murder. First Nations people gained the right to vote in federal elections. The status of women was recognized with a Royal Commission. Canadian musical taste shifted from Don Messer to the Guess Who, from "Our Pet" Juliette to Joni Mitchell.

Canada was, as someone put it, "a nation in search of itself." In 1951, the report of the Massey Commission railed against American influence on Canadian culture. In its wake, we saw the creation of institutions such as the Canada Council charged with promoting a distinctive Canadian identity. On the international stage, led by Lester Pearson's key role as an intermediary in settling the Suez Crisis in 1956, an achievement for which he was awarded the Nobel Peace Prize, Canada was emerging from the shadow of both its mother and its neighbour to establish a reputation as a peacemaker and leader among middle powers.

On the football field, it was also a time of transition, a defining period in the history of the game. At its inception, players sported leather helmets. By the end, they would be indistinguishable, to a casual observer, from players today. Except they were smaller. A big running back in the 1940s might go five-ten, 185 pounds. A rare lineman who stood six-foot-four or -five was a Goliath among pygmies.

As the era began, the game itself was different, too. An unconverted touchdown counted for only 5 points. Player positions bore arcane names like "flying wing" and "snap." In many respects, Canadian football still bore a resemblance to its parent sport of rugby.

Accounts of a game called football date back to the 1860s, with the University of Toronto claiming to have first hosted the sport on November 9, 1861. Amateur clubs sprouted soon after in the cities of the East. Canadian football's oldest rivalry was inaugurated on October 18, 1873, when the Hamilton Foot Ball Club, sporting yellow and black jerseys for the first time, fell scoreless to the blue-sweatered Toronto Argonauts at the University of Toronto grounds. Hamilton fans have yet to get over it.

The essence of the Canadian game was the innovation of John Thrift Meldrum Burnside, a former captain of the Toronto varsity squad, who drew up a set of rules that distinguished our game not only from rugby but also from the version of football developing south of the border. These stipulated, among other things, twelve men to a side, and the objective of gaining 10 yards on 3 downs. With their adoption in 1903, modern Canadian football was born.

In the late 1940s, football's governing body was still called the Canadian Rugby Union. Ontario Rugby Football Union teams from small centres, like the Sarnia Imperials and the Kitchener-Waterloo Dutchmen, still contended against the big-city teams of the "Big Four" (as the Interprovincial Rugby Football Union was known), like the Montreal Alouettes or the Toronto Argonauts, for the right to represent the East in the Grey Cup. Sarnia had won the Cup as recently as 1936.

Relations between the eastern teams and the teams of the Western Interprovincial Football Union, which in the late forties consisted only of teams in Winnipeg, Calgary and Regina, were as frosty and argumentative as those between eastern and western Canadians in any other form of endeavour. But, as in Confederation itself, each recognized the necessity of the others if any were to survive. Talks began regarding rationalization of rules and the possibility of some interlocking play, although the Canadian Football League itself would not come into existence until 1958.

It may seem incredible today, when a natural assumption prevails that the world's best football is played in the National Football League, but in the 1940s and 1950s, even into the 1960s, the level of play on both sides of the border was comparable. At the end of the 1940s, when it was struggling to digest the remnants of the failed All-America Football Conference, and in the early sixties, when it was contending with the upstart American Football League, the NFL was vulnerable to raiding by Canadian clubs. Statistics for a standout of the Canadian game such as Sam Etcheverry or Ron Lancaster compare favourably with those of an NFL legend like Sammy Baugh or Johnny Unitas.

In Canada, whether they hailed from north or south of the border, players became part of the community in which they played. Most players were fairly well compensated for what amounted to a few months' part-time work, but only the stars made more than a living wage. What the teams offered instead was part-time employment off the field, often in jobs provided by team boosters who were willing to make liberal allowance for a player's absence from the workplace during football season.

In addition to earning them a bit more spending money, this arrangement allowed players the opportunity to build a career that they could step into full time once their playing days were over. Hometown heroes could parlay their prominence in football into financial opportunities that would not otherwise have been open to them. American players would arrive in town, planning to stay a few years and then bolt for the border. More often than not, they would meet a local girl, get involved in business ventures, then settle down for good. For many players from small-town America, a compact city like Calgary or Winnipeg was much more congenial than Chicago or New York.

Above all, the Grey Cup game in that era was an obsession for all Canadian sports fans, east and west. It was a time each year when they put aside petty regional differences, like economic inequality or freight rates, and settled in front of their radios or television sets to bear witness to an event of truly national significance. Like the Jews and the Philistines, they were content, for one afternoon each year, to cease their striving and leave the battlefield to their champions to settle the issue.

Football fans across the nation would throw Grey Cup parties for friends and family, serving fare prepared from recipes featured in the Food section of the daily paper. Special trains and chartered flights would converge on the host city (usually Toronto), spewing forth bevies of well-lubricated, enthusiastic supporters of the contending teams (almost always *not* the Argos).

The Grey Cup parade would draw shivering hordes of spectators to the streets to cheer on the majorettes and marching bands, festooned floats and tail-finned convertibles with Miss Grey Cup contestants perched on top. The night before the game, tolerant police would ignore the spirited hijinks of strolling celebrants, occasionally spiced by the odd riot.

In those faraway days, Canadian football filled the sports pages over the autumn months. Hockey season was barely underway, its first games without drama or importance. Besides, there were only the two Canadian teams in the NHL, the Leafs and the Canadiens. Box lacrosse had a higher profile than hockey in some cities of the West. The World Series lacked relevance for many Canadians. News of the NFL might serve as filler; the NBA, a fringe roundball league, would seldom surface.

Football was it. It satisfied the head and the heart, with its strategy and its striving. It was, as Vancouver sportswriter Jim Kearney termed it, "chess with muscles." By the mid-1950s, there were teams from coast to coast. Television spread the message into every nook and cranny of the nation. Every major city had its hometown heroes, whose exploits were the focus of the Monday morning quarterback crowd at the barbershop or coffee counter. Fans were buoyed by each victory; they sagged with each defeat. Records were set that would stand for decades.

Nowadays, as the very survival of the league is in doubt, when the future of its franchises appears to be as farm teams for the NFL, it is timely to remember what Canadian football once was. That is not to say that today's league does not feature some exceptional players. The size, strength, athleticism and perhaps even the technical proficiency of today's players is, without question, superior to that of players of the postwar quarter-century.

But there is a qualitative difference between statistics and legends, between efficiency and glory. One is a creature of the cranium, the other of the imagination. One engages your attention, the other, your soul. It is in pursuit of that distinction that we offer this book.

CHAPTER ONE

The Last of the Leather-Helmets:
Toronto Argonauts

The King sat on his wooden throne, holding his leather crown in his powerful hands. He sat alone because he was not serving. He was not needed. He was not wanted. This is not the way great kings abdicate, but this is the way Joe Krol's reign ended: not with a bang but with a benching.

It was November 29, 1952, and time was running out on the Grey Cup game. In Toronto's Varsity Stadium, 27,391 spectators, a total sellout, were howling with happiness as the Toronto Argos played out what would be a 21-11 victory over the Edmonton Eskimos, the eighth national title for the skilled team in the blue-on-blue uniforms.

But there was no joy at the end of the Argonaut bench where Joe "King" Krol sat, his double-blue sweater scarcely smudged. The greatest

Argo of them all, one of the greatest all-round players in the history of the game, the hero of three straight Argo Grey Cup victories in the late 1940s, had become a scrub. His skills diminished, his value discounted, he was used this Grey Cup afternoon only as a punter, dutifully loping onto the field on third down, booting the ball high and deep, then returning to his inglorious seat on the bench as younger men did all the running, passing and catching that he used to do.

There was deep significance to the image of Krol and his diminished importance to the Argos. The last of the great leather-helmets was being phased out, and Canadian football was embarking on a profound, wrenching change: it was putting a premium on imported American players and relegating homegrown Canadians, who had been the heart, the lifeblood and the soul of the game since it began, to a minor, roster-filling role.

The presence of American players had been a bone the eastern and western franchises had growled over since early in the century. Before the Second World War, the East had assumed the ethical high ground, decrying the West's reliance on imported talent. But in the years after the war, the eastern teams helped erode the Canadian nature of the game. Frank Cosentino, in his book *Canadian Football: The Grey Cup Years*, relates that Joe Ryan, a Montreal Alouettes shareholder, when introducing a motion at the 1946 Canadian Rugby Union annual general meeting that would allow each team to field five imports, "stated that he thought that the Canadian discrimination against imports 'was born of panic and provincialism.' " Steadfast in opposition was the Argos' bantam-cock head coach Teddy Morris. But the motion passed; within a decade the limit would be upped to seven and beyond. And by 1952, Morris was gone, and Krol was fading away.

Joe Krol came to the professional game in 1943, but they heard him coming long before that. As a king-in-waiting preppie at Windsor-Kennedy Collegiate he won twelve varsity letters before moving on to play so brilliantly at the University of Western Ontario that the Detroit Lions invited him to their training camp. The Lions let him get away, though. Annis Stukus, another Argo star of all-round talent, recalls the Detroit decision. "I went down to the Detroit camp and asked the coach, Gus Dorais, what he thought of Krol. He told me, 'The only faster guy in camp than Krol is an NCAA sprint champion. He does everything. He's the best runner and the best passer we've got and the best kicker I've ever seen. I'm cutting him next week. He doesn't have the right kind of discipline.' "

Jim Coleman, who began covering Canadian football in 1931, says today, "I first heard of Krol when he was the schoolboy phenom of Ontario. He was a great all-round athlete and a great player in the Argos' great years. Whether it was Krol passing to Royal Copeland or Copeland passing to Krol, they were the devil to defend. Krol was a marvellous kicker, he ran like a striped-ass ape and was a powerful runner and passer. I still think Jackie Parker was the greatest we've ever seen in Canada, but Krol and Hal Patterson were close to him. Joe loved football as a game, but he never approached it as a war. So, yes, he could be lackadaisical at times."

Dorais did indeed cut Krol, who went home to Windsor and sat by his telephone. It was a week before the Argos called, made an offer and set a legend in motion. Krol joined the Argos in time for their sixth game of the season, in Montreal, and made a quick impression, throwing 4 touchdown passes to Royal Copeland and kicking 2 singles and 2 converts. Copeland also tossed a touchdown pass in the game, and Montreal writers nicknamed the Krol-Copeland duo the "Gold Dust Twins." From then on, Krol and Copeland alternated at tailback and quarterback in the Argos' single-wing formation, giving them the flexibility to throw passes to each other. They formed a deadly combination when given their head by coach Teddy Morris. They won the Grey Cup three years in a row—1945, 1946 and 1947—as Krol wrote indelible scoring numbers.

On December 1, 1945, just weeks after they celebrated the end of the Second World War, 19,000 Canadian football fans jammed Varsity Stadium to watch the first peacetime Grey Cup final in the better part of a decade. The same day, across the border in Philadelphia, 100,002 Americans, including President Harry Truman, took in the Army-Navy game. With the real fighting over, North Americans could afford themselves the luxury of renewing domestic rivalries: East vs. West, Cadets vs. Middies, great battles in which territory could be taken and lost without the loss of life.

In the middle of the war, when things looked darkest for the Allied Forces in Europe, the Western Interprovincial Football Union and the eastern Big Four had suspended operations. For the duration, the Grey Cup had been played, but the combatants were service teams—the Toronto RCAF Hurricanes, the Winnipeg RCAF Bombers, the Hamilton Flying Wildcats and the Montreal–St-Hyacinthe–Donnacona Navy— and the matches were staged events designed to bolster the nation's morale. Now, with the players back in civvies, the national struggle could be resumed.

The 1945 cup final reinforced East-West antagonisms with a vengeance as the Argos, on touchdowns by Krol and Copeland, plus 2 each from Doug Smylie—fresh from the service, where he had been heavyweight boxing champion of the RCAF—and Billy Myers, shut down Winnipeg 35-0. Not once did the Bombers get beyond the Argo 50-yard line.

The following year, the Bombers improved somewhat—but not enough. Winnipeg managed to score 1 touchdown, by quarterback Wally Dobler on a 2-yard sneak, and they held the Argos to 4 touchdowns, from Krol, Copeland, Doug Smylie's younger brother Rod, who had been shot down over Europe flying another sort of bomber, and bruising Byron Karrys. The Karrys score, on a 1-yard blast, came after Krol lofted a high punt that Copeland, who had been lined up on-side, ran under and caught on the 1-yard line, outjumping two Winnipeg defenders. Krol completed 7 of 13 passes, 3 for touchdowns, and kicked 3 converts, as the Argos won 28-6 to further chafe western pride.

The irritation was not eased in 1947. The Bombers sulked into the dressing room at the final whistle, convinced they had been jobbed. The incident was an apparent third-quarter touchdown pass from Winnipeg's Bob Sandberg to Johnny Reagan, which was called back after officials ruled that Reagan had not been over the line of scrimmage when he caught the ball. Under the rules of the day, that made it an illegal pass. "I'd bet my life I was over the line of scrimmage on the play," groused Reagan after the game. "I turned around to see what was going on in our backfield and the ball came to me." The call unsettled the Bombers, who at one point had a 9-0 lead. But the ruling and the rattling let the Argos back in. They tied it late in the last quarter on a single by Krol. Then, after Sandberg gambled on a fake-kick plunge that did not get first-down yardage, the Bombers turned the ball over. With three seconds on the clock, Krol, from the Bomber 48-yard line, lofted an angled punt in and out of the corner of the Winnipeg end zone for a single and a 10-9 victory. Krol was in on all the Toronto points. He passed to Copeland for a touchdown, converted and added 3 points on rouges before his game-winning kick.

Exhaustion may have been a factor in the third straight Winnipeg loss—they used only fifteen players, most of them going both ways for sixty minutes—but Krol was the killer they couldn't stop. That's why they called him King Krol: he didn't just play well, he *reigned*. He forbade defeat. He played for six Grey Cup winners. Twice he was named Canada's athlete of the year. In all his Argo years, Krol scored 291 points—and this was the era of the five-point touchdown, an era when individual record-keeping was lax. His recorded Grey Cup points total alone was 30. These totals still rank him second in career Argo scoring (specialist kickers excepted).

Joe Krol was the killer they couldn't stop. That's why they called him King Krol: he didn't just play well, he <u>reigned.</u>

The passage of half a century has not dulled the lustre of Krol's accomplishments. Annis Stukus recalled in 1997, "Krol was just a goddamned great athlete. People forget that he was six-foot-two, 220 pounds. On top of that he had a great mind that made him a great success in business after football. As an athlete, he was in a class by himself. He could have played major league baseball and hit .350. He'd have been a great point guard in pro basketball. If he had learned to skate, he would have made the NHL." In 1987, Toronto sportswriter-historian Gord Walker wrote glowingly, "Even dictionaries have trouble providing the right words to describe how great was the young man who burst onto the Canadian football scene in 1943. Boiled down to basics, Joe Krol was a winner, maybe the best ever in Canada when the chips were down. The more challenging the situation, the better he resolved it."

Joe Krol may have been known as the King, but he was simply the last in a regal lineage that stretched back into the misty origins of Canadian football. Long before there were Toronto Maple Leafs, there were Toronto Argonauts. In 1872, a grand traditionalist named Henry O'Brien formed a Toronto rowing club, dressing his several crews in the light blue of Cambridge and the dark blue of Oxford. Two years later, the club sponsored a rugby football team and, but for the rude interruptions of two world wars, the double-blue has graced Canadian football fields ever since. Generations of sportswriters have developed furrowed brows trying to conjure up alternatives for the proper term, "Argonauts"— "Scullers," "Oarsmen," "Boatmen."

The Argonauts played in the first East-West Grey Cup football final in December 1921, defeating Edmonton 23-0 before 9,558 spectators as Lionel Conacher, the Big Train, highballed for 3 touchdowns. Toronto-based teams have won twenty-one Grey Cups: four by the University of Toronto team between 1909 and 1920; one wartime championship by the Toronto RCAF Hurricanes; two by the charmingly named Toronto Balmy Beach, in 1927 and 1930, and thirteen by the Argos between 1914 and 1996.

That might indicate a dynasty, but instead, it would be more accurate to describe the Argonauts as a series of events highlighted by a succession of phenomena: phenomena like the Big Train, Red Storey, the Stukii, Sonshine's Folly, the Ballad of Leo Cahill and the Argo Bounce.

Lionel Conacher. The Big Train. Now there was a legend, in life and in death. In 1950 he was named Canada's greatest male athlete of the half century and, really, there were no serious competitors. Conacher could not hear of a sport without trying it and, usually, dominating it. He was the Canadian light-heavyweight boxing champion and, just to see if he could do it, he went four rounds against Jack Dempsey. He played for nine Canadian championship field lacrosse teams. He played twelve seasons in the National Hockey League, an uncompromisingly tough defenceman. In baseball, he played in the Little World Series with the Toronto Maple Leafs. They put a clock on him in a baseball uniform, and he ran a 10.4 100 yards. He was a straight-ahead, smash-face plunger with the Argonauts, no guile, no feinting, just bone and strength against stacked defences. He scored 15 points in his one Grey Cup game with the Argos in 1921.

Conacher paid the full price for his playing style. His nose was broken eight times. He broke an arm and both legs, cracked seven ribs. They put two hundred stitches in his face and sixteen to close up a serious cut near his jugular vein. But none of this stopped him, or even slowed him down. In 1954, long after his retirement from paid sports, Conacher became the Liberal member of Parliament for Toronto Trinity. In a softball game between members and the press gallery, the fifty-four-year-old Conacher cracked a line drive to centre field. It would have been a double for any other middle-aged man, but Conacher stretched it into a triple. He dusted himself off on third base, smiled, and then dropped dead. The Big Train had made its last stop.

Red Storey's football career was quick, but it was large. He played less than three seasons before serious injuries forced him into other work, including becoming a great National Hockey League referee and a sought-after banquet speaker. But Storey was a giant black headline in newspapers all across Canada the day after the December 10, 1938, Grey Cup game between Toronto and Winnipeg. Storey was a big, raw-boned redhead from Barrie, Ontario, and for three quarters of the 1938 final, he was an idle cipher, hoping to get into the game long enough to dirty his spotless sweater. He got in as a fourth-quarter sub for the injured Doug McPherson, with Winnipeg leading Toronto 7-6. In the next fifteen minutes he scored 3 touchdowns and missed a fourth by one inch. He simply picked up that Toronto team in his big, freckled hands and carried them to a stunning 30-7 victory.

His first score came on a blistering 28-yard run that put Toronto ahead 11-7. In Storey's words: "I was the middle man on an end run and Bob Isbister let me loose. Art Wheat was the wide man and I faked a lateral to him. Then I cut over tackle and ran all the way in." Next, Storey intercepted a pass and returned it 40 yards to the end zone. Then he took part in another interception. "Isbister really set me up. He intercepted the ball on our 2-yard line and lateraled to me. I galloped 100 yards before someone knocked me out of bounds on the one-inch line. Bill Stukus threw a touchdown pass to Bernie Thornton on the next play." Storey's third touchdown was a 20-yard run. "I forget who opened the hole but it was a beauty," he recalled.

One of Annis Stukus's fondest boasts is that he played at offensive end that game and "threw the blocks on two of Storey's touchdowns. I wrapped up that big Bud Marquardt and Red ran in off my fanny."

Annis, Bill and Frank called themselves the Stukii, the Lithuanian plurality of athletic Stukus brothers who were a virtual committee of talent on Toronto Argonaut teams in the thirties. They kept coming to the Argos like a series of gifts from Mother Stukus: Annis in 1935, Bill in 1936 and Frank in 1938.

Annis recalls, "We were healthy, husky kids because our mother raised us on meatball soup. From the time we were infants until we left home, our mother had this great big pot simmering on the back of the stove. Every bone, every scrap of meat, every leftover vegetable went into the pot. Every week she'd toss in a handful of fresh meatballs. We'd come home from school on a cold afternoon, have a bowl of soup and go out and throw a football until it got dark. Three hundred and sixty-five days a year my brothers and I threw a football around, winter and summer. Hot days and in the snow, we threw the ball. We learned to throw it the right way. By the time we were ten, we knew how to look left, throw to the right, and we knew how to catch it. You could always tell a Stukus boy. We were the ones with the back pockets of our pants torn off from playing rough touch football.

The Stukii, the Lithuanian plurality of athletic Stukus brothers, were a virtual committee of talent on the Argos.

"I was coaching my first team when I was ten. We lived on one side of Trinity Park. There were a bunch of guys on the other side of the park who thought they were tough. I put a team together, so did they, and we showed them who was tough. When we were with the Argos, I sometimes made up plays in the huddle, triple laterals, halfback passes to the quarterback, that we had used on our ten-year-olds team."

All three of the Stukii graduated from the Argo juniors to the senior team, and none had to endure any growing pains in the pros; they knew their fundamentals. In 1938 they became the only three brothers in Canadian football history to play in the same Grey Cup–winning backfield. On November 5 of that year, the Stukus family compact scored 4 touchdowns in a 58-13 massacre of Montreal. Bill passed to Annis for a score, Annis passed to Frank for a touchdown, and Bill ran for 2 other majors. It had never happened before; it's unlikely to happen again.

Annis was twenty when he joined the Argos with seven other graduates of the junior team. All eight of them made the big club, and three years later they were in the Grey Cup. Annis was the Argos' backfield coach at twenty-three, an all-East quarterback, and in 1936, his second season as a pro, he started at seven different positions, including centre, or "snap" as it was called in those days.

Football came easily to Annis. What was not easy was his testy relationship with Argo coach Lew Hayman, the dapper American from Syracuse who would spend thirty-eight years in Canadian football as a coach, manager and team owner in Toronto and Montreal and was the first coach to win five Grey Cups.

"Hayman was a great guy for getting a team ready, but once the game began, we wished we could lock him up," says Stukus. "He killed us with his four-hour practices. The Wednesday night practices were like war; the survivors got to play on Saturday. I have always believed that smart coaches listen to advice from players. It wasn't until I started coaching the backfield that Hayman began to believe in me.

"In that 1938 Grey Cup game against Winnipeg, the Bombers dressed fourteen Americans. We dressed one and we benched him after the first three minutes. We were really going badly at the start of the last quarter. Bill was playing quarterback, I was playing end. I told Bill to start calling the plays that we had run as kids, the long triple laterals. Bill said he was waiting for Hayman to call them. I said, 'Call them now or I'll punch you out.' So he did and that set Storey loose for his 3 touchdowns that won it for us."

Annis Stukus merits his place in the Canadian Football Hall of Fame as a player and as a builder of two successful franchises, in Edmonton and Vancouver. Perhaps there should also be a shelf reserved in the hall for Mrs. Stukus's soup pot.

For three-quarters of a century, the arms and the legs, the heart and the soul of the Argos' many successes had been Canadian talent. Their heroes—Conacher, Storey, the Stukii, Krol and Copeland—were home-bred. Their head coach in the late 1940s, Teddy Morris, was an outspoken opponent of the "Americanization" of the game. Canadian football ought to be played by Canadians, he felt. In leading Toronto to three straight postwar Grey Cups, Morris had lived up to his convictions, fielding an all-Canadian, no-import lineup. But by the second half of the twentieth century, team owners were selling foreign glamour and emptying their shelves of homegrown products. The Argos went along to stay along, discarding Morris before the 1950 season and bringing in a tall, sombre man named Frank Clair.

Clair had played as an end at Ohio State, then professionally with the Washington Redskins, and he learned coaching at the boots of two brilliant teachers, Paul Brown and Sid Gillman. Conservative by nature, Clair was a football reformer. Although he had never seen a Canadian football game before he was hired, the first thing he did on coming to Toronto was to throw out the run-oriented single-wing and install the T-formation. Joe Krol became a backup to a runty, howitzer-armed import quarterback named Nobby. Royal Copeland was traded to Calgary.

Not that Krol didn't see it coming. A lover of the old rugby football traditions, he wrote an article in *Maclean's* in 1949, sounding the alarm. Under the headline "They're Ruining Rugby," Krol wrote, "The process has been hastened by the steady stream of American reading material which glorifies the U.S. gridiron here. I think even our radio commentators are unwittingly strengthening the trend by the use of American terminology." Almost a half-century later, Krol's words would be used by others in higher places in reaction to the threat the American mass media posed to Canada's entire culture.

While Clair kissed off the time-proven skills and leadership of Krol, he did get some instant success from two import quarterbacks he scouted and signed, Norbert "Nobby" Wirkowski from the University of Miami (Ohio) and Al Dekdebrun. Dekdebrun, a former Buffalo Bills quarterback, came up a genius in the 1950 Winnipeg-Toronto Grey Cup game, the infamous Mud Bowl. Varsity Stadium was covered by a thick snowfall the week of the final. A temperature rise just before the game caused the heavy-duty snow removal equipment to sink into the rapidly thawing field. Before the eyes of the 27,000 fans who anted up a $65,000 gate, the melt produced mud, inches of thick, clinging mud that neutralized the passing game of the much-vaunted Bomber import quarterback, "Indian" Jack Jacobs, who played so poorly that in the fourth quarter he was replaced by a young Canadian, Pete Petrow. Two Jacobs fumbles led to a pair of Toronto field goals by Nick Volpe. A Jacobs punt was blocked, leading to the game's only touchdown, on a short sneak by Dekdebrun. Another punt slipped off the side of Jacobs's foot and caromed off umpire Cliff Riseborough's head into touch. A few days after Toronto's 13-0 victory, Dekdebrun revealed why he had had only minimal trouble handling the greasy ball. He had taped thumbtacks to the palm and thumb of his right hand, snipping off the points so as not to puncture the ball, giving him a good grip for handoffs and the ability to put a spiral on the ball on the only 3 passes he threw during the ball game. Krol came off the bench just long enough to kick 2 singles, although his deep punts helped Toronto gain territorial advantage.

In Krol's last full season, 1952, he was relegated, more often than not, to the sidelines. The Toronto team did go to the Grey Cup. Wirkowski scored 1 touchdown and passed for another in the Argonauts' 21-11 victory over Edmonton. Argonaut management celebrated, but they didn't hear the sound of a curtain falling. A Toronto team would not make the Grey Cup for another nineteen years.

When kings step down, by choice or by force, empires often crumble. And so it was in Toronto. After Krol left in 1952—he tried to come back in 1955, but he was thirty-five years old, he'd been to too many banquets, and he didn't have it any more—the Argos would not win another Grey Cup game until 1983.

In relation to the problems that would plague Argo teams over the decades, Harry Sonshine was a momentary irritation, a quick flea bite. But that bite festered and almost unleashed a plague of war between Canada and the United States.

Sonshine had played three seasons with the Argos in the late 1930s, his career unique only in that he played without a helmet—which may help explain later developments. A hustler, a hard worker, a very persuasive talker, Sonshine became a self-made millionaire in the manufacturing business, while staying close to the Argos as an influential hanger-on who loved travelling with the team, eating with the players, having access to the dressing room.

At the start of the 1954 season, Argo management expressed concern that season-ticket revenue was down; there seemed to be a fan perspective that the team was old, dull and without glamour. Sonshine, who had ingratiated himself with those at the executive table, gave the opinion that poor scouting was the problem. He'd like to change all that, he said. Incredibly, the hand-wringing executives gave Sonshine not just a quiet go-ahead, but a $100,000 scouting fund.

The 1954 Argos finished out of the playoffs, and from out of the bushes Sonshine pounced. In mid-December, he announced the firing of all thirteen Argonaut imports. Frank Clair quit in protest. Sonshine went out of town, came back and announced he had signed contracts from eight American players, most of whom were still under NFL contracts. Sonshine, throwing around the Argos' hundred grand, had offered the players more money than they were getting from their current teams, which convinced them to bolt for Canada. The reaction was explosive. The NFL threatened everything short of closing the border. Tim Mara of the New York Giants told reporters, "We'll drive those Canadians out of business." The other Canadian teams deplored Sonshine's tactics, saying his approach would price players out of their reach and result in murderous legal wars with the NFL.

The Big Four met in an emergency session and tried to negate the eight contracts. Eventually, they backed down halfway and allowed Sonshine to bring in Tom Dublinksi, Billy Shipp, Bill Allbright and Gil Mains. Sonshine raided the New York Giants staff and signed Bill Swiacki as the Argos' head coach. The threatened border war faded, and the 1955 Argos, replete with Sonshine's hand-picked heroes, finished 4-8. In the resulting disarray, Toronto publisher John Bassett and the eternal Lew Hayman purchased the football team from the Argonaut Rowing Club, and Harry Sonshine disappeared over the horizon.

So, unfortunately, did the fortunes of the Argonauts. From the mid-1950s to the mid-1960s, the team endured six changes at head coach, six changes in coaching philosophy and football strategy that left the players' heads spinning. From 1956 through 1966, they averaged a woeful four wins a year, except in 1960, an aberration, when they went 10-4 to win the East before falling to Ottawa in the eastern final. This solitary blip on the otherwise flat-line heart monitor of the Argos was engineered by head coach Lou Agase and driven by league-leading efforts from receiver Dave Mann, running back Cookie Gilchrist and especially quarterback Tobin Rote, the latter on the downslide of a brilliant career that had seen him star with the Detroit Lions. Determined to prove that he still had what it took, Rote passed for 7 touchdowns in a game *twice* that year, as the Argos romped 50-15 and 63-27 over the Montreal Alouettes, and Rote thumbed his nose at his personal rival, Als quarterback Sam Etcheverry. In the second game, Cookie Gilchrist scored 27 points on 3 touchdowns, 8 converts and a single to clinch the CFL scoring title by one point over Winnipeg's Gerry James.

One constant glimmer in an otherwise dim era was the play of eight-time all-star running back Dick Shatto, whose 91 career touchdowns is still third best in the history of the league. An often-gruff Tobin Rote, late in the 1960 season, positively gushed about Shatto's talent. "Shatto's our guy," he said. "He is one of the best halfbacks I've ever seen. Dick can do so much. He can run up the middle, or off tackle, or sweep wide. He can catch passes short or deep. And block. Nobody broke through on me all year when Dick was my pass blocker." The reporter wondered if Rote thought Shatto could cut it in the National Football League. "Could Shatto play in the NFL? Man, he could *star* in the NFL."

But despite their wealth of talent, the Argos were outpointed in the eastern final by an Ottawa team that had a couple of young quarterbacks on its roster—one named Jackson, the other Lancaster. The next year, the Toronto team slipped to 7-6, and two years later, the Argos were back to their woeful ways, finishing the season at 4-10 and setting the stage for the arrival of Leo Cahill.

Leo Cahill was fun, entertaining, endearing. Even when Argo fans tired of him, they didn't abuse or ignore him.

The one thing Cahill did that a truckful of other unsuccessful Argonaut coaches had never done was to make losing relatively palatable. Leo was fun, he was entertaining, he was endearing. Even when Argo fans tired of him, they didn't abuse him or ignore him. They came to the ballpark in their tens of thousands and sang "Good-bye, Leo" to him— an affectionate if ironic sentiment that they half-hoped they would never see fulfilled.

Cahill's life seemed to be a series of traumas and disappointments eased by his Irish sense of humour. Toronto writer Jay Teitel described him vividly: "Leo Cahill was a gremlin. He was a leprechaun. He even looked a bit to me like a leprechaun, a well-fed, plump-faced, boyish refugee from *Finian's Rainbow*, wearing a pair of tinted glasses . . . He was an Irish hustler with a hustler's magical touch for discovery; a consummate PR director who wore his heart on his sleeve, a vulnerable confidence man full of bluff and schtick and contradictions."

In his book *For Love, Money and Future Considerations*, former Argo all-star pass receiver Mel Profit said Argo players often wondered about Cahill's emotional stability, but Profit, as were the others, was always charmed by Cahill's ability to turn phrases like an Irish novelist. When Cahill wanted to fire a player who had displeased him, he would call the player and instruct, "Go out that door, turn right, head for the lake and keep walking until your hat floats." A short running back, to Cahill, had to "stand on two bricks to kick a duck in the ass." In a contract session, Cahill told Profit, "Last year you turned from sugar to shit and now you're asking for that kind of money!"

It seemed as if Cahill's entire life had prepared him for life as an Argo coach. He has said that all he ever wanted to be was the reincarnation of Knute Rockne leading Notre Dame. But Cahill couldn't even play for Notre Dame, let alone coach them. The Irish weren't recruiting 170-pound linemen in the 1940s, so Cahill went to the University of Illinois as a guard and played for their 1947 Rose Bowl winner. Then the U.S Army got in the way. Cahill was drafted and shipped to Korea. One night 137 members of a rifle company in the First Cavalry Division went out on manoeuvres. Only seven of them came back alive or without wounds. One of them was rifleman Leo Cahill. After that, everything in life got easier, including a series of low-paying assistant coaching jobs at U.S. colleges, until Perry Moss brought Cahill to Canada as a member of the Montreal Alouettes staff. Then Cahill coached the Montreal Rifles—and, when they moved, the Toronto Rifles—of the Continental League. The Rifles were a two-year sensation under Cahill's imaginative coaching, and the Argos simply had to bring him in, whether for his coaching skills or his marketing genius or his genuine popularity.

Cahill's Argos were "verge" teams; they were constantly on the verge of becoming national champions, but always some curse, perhaps Irish in origin, blind-sided them. But it seemed the 1971 Argo team was just too good to be stopped by bad mojo. Cahill had a powerhouse team. He had the streakily brilliant Joe Theismann, a Heismann Trophy winner at Notre Dame, at quarterback, with Greg Barton backing him up, Profit and Bobby Taylor catching passes, Dick Thornton at defensive back, massive Jim Stillwagon at tackle, the graceful Bill Symons at one running back and the colossal rookie Leon McQuay, the Schenley Award runner-up, at the other running back.

This was the first Argo team in a decade to win the East. They beat Hamilton in the eastern final and headed to Vancouver for the Grey Cup game. But even as the Argos were packing, massive rainclouds were building up on the coastal mountains and evil spirits were chuckling at Empire Stadium where, for the first time in league history, a Grey Cup game would be played on artificial turf. What west-coast people refer to as a "Prince Rupert skullbuster" inundated the stadium all week. Despite its all-weather claims, the artificial turf couldn't handle that much water, so it just collected it.

Late in the game, the defence-oriented Calgary Stampeders held a 14-11 lead over the Argos in a nondescript game, and it seemed just a matter of killing the clock a few minutes more before the Calgary team could get back in the locker room and empty their boots. But Calgary's Jerry Keeling, a very good defensive back and an adequate quarterback, made one of those mistakes that can haunt men to their graves: he threw a high-risk pass in a play-safe situation. Thornton, who had always wanted to be a quarterback, made a brilliant interception and seemed on his way to a 60-yard touchdown when Keeling, the last man available, brought him down on the Stampeder 14-yard line with a hundred seconds on the clock.

It seemed the gods were smiling on Leo Cahill. A field goal would tie it, and the Argos could win in overtime. All they had to do was put the ball in front of the posts for kicker Ivan MacMillan. But they were not allowing for the "Argo Bounce."

For half a century, Canadian football writers have been writing about the Argo Bounce. They have never adequately described it; indeed, they have never unanimously agreed whether it is a good thing or a bad, a blessing or a curse, a positive or a negative influence on Argonaut football luck.

Some of the really old writers can describe specifically weird bounces: fumbled balls bouncing right back into the hands of Argo fumblers; bad punts taking fortuitous hops, all to the good of the Argos. Ironically, there was a classic example of the Argo Bounce in the 1996 Grey Cup final, Toronto against Edmonton. In the fourth quarter of a tight game played in a blizzard, Toronto quarterback Doug Flutie kept the ball on a desperate short-yardage play. Television pictures showed clearly that he lost the ball and didn't make the necessary yardage. But the ball bounced back to him and officials made a careless measurement, giving Toronto the vital first down to maintain possession. The Argo Bounce, surely. But no one on the broadcast team invoked the expression. Most likely, they were too young to have heard it used in that way.

In his witty book *The Argo Bounce*, Jay Teitel managed to put some metaphysical spin on the negative interpretation the Bounce received during the Argos' decades in the wilderness. He wrote, "To an Argo fan born during the post-war baby-boom . . . the Argo Bounce has moved to the metaphorical, to the description of the Argos' lack of fortune in general. The Bounce can be used as a synonym for the hex or jinx or 'demon of the past' . . . A crazy piece of strategy, an obscure rule that crops up perversely in a game's final moments, a terrible player deal, a baffling comment by a coach whose team is 0 and 8 . . . Where the fans of most losing teams have to make do with generalities, Argo fans can always without hesitation blame the Argo Bounce."

On that soggy Vancouver day in November 1971, Joe Theismann, a gritty competitor accustomed to winning, set up behind centre, the game on the line. Symons gained 4 on first down. On second down, Theismann handed off to Leon McQuay, sweeping left. McQuay's job was to go down when he saw the middle of the posts. But McQuay was struck with inspiration. He saw, or thought he saw, a golden path of open space leading into the end zone and, instead of going down sensibly, he tried to cut to the glory hole. His wheels spun on the surface water, he lost his balance, and he lost the ball.

Calgary recovered. Calgary held through the agony of the dying seconds. The Argos had bounced again.

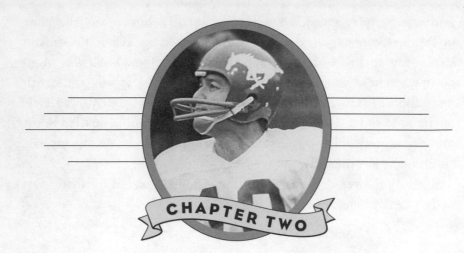

CHAPTER TWO

Hot Time in the Old Town:
Calgary Stampeders

From the time the Ice Age glaciers retreated, through the nomadic visits of Blackfoot, Sarcee and Stoney hunters, the spot had waited over ten thousand years for someone to come by and stay.

On a blazing hot summer day in 1875, a saddle-sore troop of North-West Mounted Police, pursuing American whiskey runners, pulled into a shaded grove of trees at the crook of the Elbow and Bow Rivers to water their mounts and wash the prairie dust out of their mouths. It was pleasantly cool there; the water was fast, cold and clean.

The commanding officer, Col. J. F. Macleod, decided it was an ideal spot for a permanent camp. He called it Fort Calgary, a Gaelic word meaning running water. Troop members toasted themselves and the land, a celebratory ritual that would become endemic in the foothills.

For those who came next and stayed to expand the campsite, the land was grateful and generous, and the tent town became a boom town. By 1901 the population was 4,400. By 1911 it had exploded to 43,700. One hundred years after Colonel Macleod planted his flag, Calgary was a city of 385,000 people. They were unique people, risk-takers who believed in sneering at failure and celebrating success. They put those characteristics into play when they embraced football as a way of prairie life.

There had been hybrid forms of rugby-football in Calgary since 1891, when Calgary and Edmonton played their first home-and-home series, kicking off a raucous provincial rivalry that hasn't cooled to this day. The Calgary Tigers were formed in 1908 but disbanded in 1914 in deference to the First War; they were replaced by the 50th Battalion and then the Calgary Altomahs. The Calgary Bronks came into being in 1935, and the team name was changed permanently to the Stampeders in 1945.

Sadly, Calgary football has never enjoyed the success of Alberta crude oil or grass-fed cattle. The franchise has won just three Grey Cups in eight tries, the Stampeders winning the national championship in 1948, 1971 and 1992. That's a long time between victory drinks.

But Calgary has left a permanent thumbprint on the silvery sides of the Grey Cup nonetheless. It is generally, though not universally, conceded that Calgarians taught Canada how to celebrate a Grey Cup game. Not as sixty minutes of football, but as seven days of hard partying, and then a football game, followed by incalculable mornings of hungover remorse. Or so legend has it.

According to the *Canadian Encyclopedia*, "Coached by Les Lear, [the Stampeders] defeated Ottawa in the 1948 Grey Cup game and the celebrations of their accompanying fans gave birth to the annual festival that has surrounded the game ever since." Tony Allan, the scholarly prairie football historian, writes in his book *Grey Cup or Bust*, "Many people say the Grey Cup final never amounted to much until a couple of train-loads of uninhibited Albertans arrived in 1948 to show staid old Toronto how the thing should be run. They certainly boosted the sales of white Stetsons if nothing else."

What Calgary football fans had done, simply, was to take the Stampede east with them. The Calgary Stampede and agricultural show had been an annual summertime fixture on the city's events calendar since 1919, drawing broncobusters, calf-ropers and bull-riders from all over North America. To show Ontario the type of he-men that lived in Calgary and to assert some territorial imperative, Calgary boosters donned their fanciest duds, loaded their hardiest broken broncos and a couple of chuckwagons onto some freight cars, partied all the way east and hit Toronto with more impact than a blizzard.

On the day before the game, more than two hundred whooping and hollering Calgary fans disgorged from their seventeen-car special train at Toronto's Union Station like a travelling company of *Oklahoma!* descending on a nunnery. To accordion accompaniment that echoed throughout the station's cavernous rotunda, they paired off and broke into an impromptu square dance. The women wore red silk blouses and sported white ten-gallon hats. The men were dressed in full cowboy gear, chaps and spurs. One twirled a lasso with which he roped locals. Another wore Stoney tribal regalia. The throng swooped across the frosty downtown street, holding up traffic for ten minutes as it advanced on the Royal York Hotel. From somewhere appeared a horse and a rider that, as the night wore on, showed up in numerous places a horse and rider are not normally expected to be. Toronto mayor Hiram McCallum, caught up in the spirit of the moment, accepted a challenge from Calgary alderman Don McKay to ride a horse down Bay Street the morning of the game. Chefs in Stetsons served up a flapjack breakfast on the steps of Toronto's old city hall. A gaggle of somewhat worse-for-the-wear cowhands in a chuckwagon led by a team of four horses and advertising the Buck Horn Guest Ranch on its canvas cover joined in the Grey Cup parade.

Still, there are dissenters to the notion that Calgary alone turned Grey Cup week into the grand national drunk that it gradually became. Muddying the waters of history, Gordon Currie wrote in his book *100 Years of Canadian Football*, "For the first time, [in 1921] the Western champions came east to fight for the Dominion championship. They were the Edmonton Eskimos, and they came with all the hoopla and spirit that has now come to be the trademark of Alberta teams."

Jim Coleman, the senior football writer in all of Canada, also hotly disputes the accepted wisdom: "I resent the idea that it was Calgary.

Winnipeg had been going to Toronto in force for years, filling two trains on each line, living four to a room in the Royal York, and they could party with anyone. The folks from Regina used to try it, but they were always broke. They were so broke that when they travelled to Toronto by train, they always hid a player or two under berths to avoid paying fares for the whole team . . . I'll admit, Calgary did give Grey Cup a new zip, but it was Winnipeg that first showed how to do a Grey Cup in style."

Whether or not its roots lay in Calgary spirit, the 1948 Grey Cup game celebration had a beneficial effect, creating a new level of popularity for Canada's national football championship. But Calgary football teams had to put up with a lot of rough sledding over many hard winters before they could grab the jug handles on the prized football trophy. Calgary had many good teams and scores of superb players, but it seemed to be Stampeder karma to leave their hottest hopes as cooling ashes on prairie playoff sites. Repeatedly, the team didn't get to challenge the nation because they kept falling down in their own back yard. Even football politics of the shabbiest kind worked against them.

In 1911, the Calgary Tigers were thwarted in their plans to go east. The Alberta, Manitoba and Saskatchewan provincial associations had combined to form the Western Canada Rugby Football Union (WCRFU) to challenge the East for the Grey Cup. The Regina Roughriders had won the first of twenty-two straight provincial championships and were to meet the Winnipeg Rowing Club for the WCRFU championship. But petrifyingly icy weather in Regina on game day forced a cancellation. Winnipeg claimed the title by default. Calgary challenged Winnipeg, beat them 13-6 and prepared to entrain east. But the Canadian Rugby Union, in a decision that smelled to the heavens, declared that the WCRFU had not been formally accepted as a CRU member in time to qualify for the national championship. Calgary was outraged. After all, the CRU had accepted and cashed the WCRFU's entry cheque.

A Calgary sportswriter blustered, "The Calgary Tigers, by virtue of their victory over the Winnipeg Rowing Club, have earned the title of Champions of Western Canada and are determined to demand a game with the winner of next Saturday's contest between the Argos and Varsity, to decide the championship of the Dominion . . . The Tigers won the championship of this league as well as the championship of Western Canada, and so must be considered before any team is declared Canadian champions."

In full-blown hauteur, the Toronto *Globe* replied, "The freshness of ignorance is responsible for the explanation by some western papers that Calgary did not get into the game because 'the Eastern Canada hog is getting in his work again.'"

In addition to the contrived excuse about the WCRFU's timing, it was well reported at the time that the bluenoses of the CRU suspected western teams of shamateurism—of directly paying players or supplying them with jobs. A *Globe* editorial sniffed, "Frank statements of some western magnates . . . indicate that they do not quite understand the amateur idea in sport. They have still to learn that a man cannot retain his amateur status if he plays football for pay. Whether in the form of a remunerative position or without any subterfuge, the effect is the same." In the end, the eastern establishment triumphed over the western upstarts, and Calgary did not get a sniff of the Grey Cup for another thirty-seven years.

Les Lear was a fanatic for conditioning. The team's daily workouts began with a mile run and calisthenics.

In 1946, with rifles being stacked in Europe and the war in the Pacific winding down, old dusty, musty football helmets were being hauled out of lockers and trunks in western Canada. Having adjourned for the duration of the war, the Western Conference held a meeting in Calgary to reconstitute itself. They would play football in 1946 but on a limited basis; only three teams, Calgary, Winnipeg and Regina, were ready to go to the post. Edmonton didn't have the resources and continued to sit out until 1949.

Calgary assembled under the guidance of coach Dean Griffing, the flamboyant American who had come north in 1936 to be Regina's playing coach. But Griffing's two-year stay in Calgary was not distinguished with tangible success, and in 1948 the Stampeders brought in Les Lear, a bigger-than-life extrovert who knew what success was all about. Lear had played in four Grey Cup games with the Winnipeg Blue Bombers and had also played with the National Football League Cleveland Rams in their championship year. That latter qualification left him with a network of great contacts in the U.S., and he nursed no nickel in recruiting experienced imports. His best were quarterback Keith Spaith and end Joe Aguirre of the professional Hawaii Warriors; Woodrow Wilson "Woody" Strode, a tall, fast end from the Los Angeles Rams; and centre Chuck Anderson, from the Los Angeles Bears. Fritzie Hanson, the twinkle-toed running back, had left Winnipeg to take a job on the Calgary Grain Exchange two years earlier and, at thirty-six, joined the Stampeders. Lear also had the veteran fullback Paul "Pappy" Rowe, who had one more good season in his old legs.

Lear was a fanatic for conditioning, putting his team through daily two-and-a-half-hour workouts that began with a mile run and thirty minutes of calisthenics. Then they scrimmaged. But Lear's greatest gift may have been his absolute faith in Canadian-born players. Eleven of them made his 1948 team, and it was a powerhouse that ran off a 12-0 season, scoring an average 17 points a game while giving up 5. Regina tied the Stampeders 4-4 in the first game of the western final, but Calgary won the second game handily to qualify for the national final against the Ottawa Rough Riders, who were overwhelming favourites to knock off Lear and his western kids.

Annis Stukus, a working newspaperman in eastern Canada at the time, recalls coming out to watch the western final and smelling upset. "Ottawa had a great team, but they were dangerously arrogant. All year they had been running on third and 15 and making it. They began to believe they were invincible. I came home from the West and wrote, 'Look out, Ottawa!'"

Eleven of the players Lear took east were eighteen- and nineteen-year olds who had come to him directly from the junior ranks. He whipped them into superb condition and worked them into his lineup as the season progressed. Four of them were running backs and receivers from Vancouver: Pete Thodos, Rod Pantages, Ced Gyles and Jim Mitchener.

Thodos, now a retired distillery executive in Vancouver, recalls, "I

played for the Meralomas; Rod, Ced and Jim played for the Vancouver
Blue Bombers. They had played in the national junior final in Calgary
and Rod got a tryout with the Stampeders. He made such an impression
that they asked him if there were any more like him at home. He gave
them our names. We all knew each other from playing junior ball at Riley
Park, and I had known Rod since we were about six. Our mothers were
the best of friends.

"So we went to camp as a group and we thought like a group. Lear was
working our asses off, but we still hadn't been offered contracts. Here's
how green we were. The four of us, plus Normie Kwong and Normie Hill,
got together one night in the Braemar Lodge. We drew straws. Rod got
the short straw so he had to phone Lear and demand a meeting. Lear
came down, saw the six of us together, smelled trouble, and told us we'd
never play organized football again. Then he stormed out. The next morning we were packing our bags to go home when the president called us and
told us to come to the office. Lear was there and ready to talk contract.

"Somehow we had got it into our heads that Frank Filchock was
making $50,000 a year. We knew we weren't as good as him, but we
figured, what the hell, maybe we're a quarter as good.

"Lear took Rod and me into the office first and asked what we
wanted. I said, 'How does $15,000 sound?'

"Lear says, 'That's not the number I had in mind.'

"I asked, 'What did you have in mind?'

"Lear says, 'Five hundred dollars.'

"I yelled, 'We'll take it! Thank you!'"

So for $3,000 plus room and board, Lear got six players who would
play dramatic roles in the 1948 Grey Cup game.

Thodos says, "Really, we just wanted to play football, and that was just
a great season. With only two other teams in the league, we played Regina
eight times, including playoffs, and Winnipeg six times. And from the
start through the Grey Cup, we didn't lose once. Spaith and Strode gave
us the best passing game in the country, and we had some great veterans,
guys like Joe Aguirre, Bert Iannone and Chick Chickowski. And after the
playoffs, there we are, a bunch of kids one year away from Riley Park,
and we're going to the Grey Cup. We went east by train and at every

single whistle stop, no matter how cold it was, Lear made us pile out of our coaches and run laps around the train."

Right up to the Grey Cup kickoff, Lear's patience was tested on and off the field. The Stampeders moved out to Appleby College, in Oakville.

"Back in those days," recalls Thodos, "using game film was illegal. But Lear had got hold of an Ottawa game film and he'd show it to us, down in the basement, right next to the coal chute. We practised hard twice a day and we took our meals at a place called the Pig & Whistle Inn. Breakfast was pretty good, but every day when we came in from a two-hour morning workout, we'd get cheese sandwiches. Day after day, cheese sandwiches. Finally, Chuck Anderson said, 'Boys, I know Lear is eating chicken and roast beef and I'm not eating another cheese sandwich.' And he walked out. One of the veterans found him in a restaurant in Toronto. It took three hours to talk him into coming back. And there were no more cheese sandwiches."

Thodos remembers that the young Stamps were annoyed to read a headline in a Toronto paper asking, "Will Lear's Kids Freeze?" "I really hated that, so when we ran out on the field for the opening kickoff, I gave the crowd the finger. Not a soul noticed."

Ottawa took a 1-0 lead in the first quarter, but Calgary went ahead 6-0 with a minute to play in the half on that mouldiest of plays, a sleeper. Thodos remembers: "Spaith had completed a pass to Strode on the sideline, and as we hurried back in the huddle, I noticed Normie Hill was missing. I'm hissing, 'Where the hell is Hill?' Aguirre, the right end, said, 'Shut up, Pete. Move in at left end.' Spaith says, 'Ball on two.' Then he winds up and throws this wobbling duck out to Hill, who is lying flat on the sideline. He has to stop, he catches it on the one, gets hit, loses the ball, falls into the end zone and catches it again flat on his back for the touchdown.

"But here's the thing. We didn't have that play in our book, we had never practised it, and it wasn't in our game plan. But on that Ottawa film we looked at in the basement, they used it. So Lear just told us to be ready for Ottawa to use it, and to check both sidelines every time they broke their huddle. We wind up using their play and scoring on it. To this day I don't know where it came from. Spaith and Hill may have been in on it, maybe Aguirre. But it came as a complete surprise to me."

The wobbling completion surprised even Spaith. "The ball felt like it had two pounds of mud stuck to it," he said at the time. "I hurried the throw and, for a second, I didn't think it would reach Normie."

Annis Stukus still savours the play: "That tells us what a great, crazy game this is. A guy in a red and white sweater and a helmet with red and white stripes is lying on green grass with 20,000 people in the seats pointing to him and yelling, 'Sleeper!' and twelve guys in Ottawa sweaters don't see him."

Calgary's second major score was just as improbable. Ottawa quarterback Bob Paffrath threw a long lateral to halfback Pete Karpuk. It was a bad toss and the ball landed at Karpuk's feet, clearly off-side. Karpuk, hearing a horn but not a whistle, ignored the ball. But Strode ambled over, picked it up and began trotting towards the Ottawa goal-line, now and then glancing over his shoulder. Eventually, two Ottawa players took after him. Strode went from mid-field to the Ottawa 13 before lateralling to Jim Mitchener, who was run out of bounds on the 10. On the next play, Thodos put a blinding move on the still-befuddled Karpuk and scored the winning touchdown in Calgary's 12-7 victory.

At the final whistle, Calgary fans surged onto the field and carried off a set of goal posts intact, bearing their trophy aloft down towards the lakeshore and setting it up inside the Royal York lobby. As the evening progressed, someone found a hand saw and began sawing off slices of the posts to sell as souvenirs for $1 apiece. A guitar-playing duo mounted a table and began belting out cowboy songs, joined enthusiastically if unmusically by the crowd. Bellboys moved quickly to spirit furniture and potted palms out of harm's way. A white-aproned maid bustled about amidst the celebrants, clucking and tutting and endeavouring to sweep up the mess before fleeing in dismay. Although boisterous, the crowd remained good-natured and not unruly. As one reporter put it, "They courteously declined to ride their horses into the elevators."

The next day, the team, their fans and their livestock left Toronto, by some reports $100,000 richer, having wagered a collective $40,000 at 8-5 odds against their heroes. The group partied all the way home in a freight car turned into a bar, $2 admission, and arrived to a civic welcome.

With all those young studs in the lineup, it looked like a Calgary dynasty. As it turned out, it was just a one-timer. By the end of the 1949 season, Calgary had run a two-year stretch of twenty-two victories and one loss in twenty-six games. But then they scraped by Saskatchewan in a tight two-game western final before losing to Montreal in the Grey Cup game. In 1950 Calgary slid to last in the West, the start of a ten-year drought in which they finished fifth twice, fourth six times and third twice. They went through five head coaches during the dry spell. The Young Turks broke up. Jim Mitchener became an outstanding brain surgeon. Ced Gyles became the chairman of the board of a major Canadian life insurance firm. Pete Thodos and Rod Pantages moved on to Montreal in 1950 and played nine seasons before retiring. Thodos is still regarded as one of the greatest kickoff-return men the game has ever seen.

With the coming of the 1960s, there was one high point for Calgary: the 1960 opening of their marvellous McMahon Stadium, totally financed by the generosity of two oil-rich citizen-sportsmen, Frank and George McMahon. It boasted a playing field below street level, 20,000 seats between the goal-lines and an open end down which swept icy north winds that tested the insulation of hardy Calgary fans.

The crowd remained good-natured. Said one reporter, "They courteously declined to ride their horses into the elevators."

The new stadium boded well for the team's future. The decline of Calgary's fortunes in the 1950s had been a combination of bad luck and bad judgement in personnel management. The Stampeders had shipped promising backs Normie Kwong and Johnny Bright to Edmonton, only to see them star in three successive Grey Cup victories. A turnaround was overdue.

It appeared to come in the 1962 season when the Stampeders finished at 9-6-1. For the next decade, they only finished under .500 once and appeared in three Grey Cup games. They acquired a thundering fullback named Earl Lunsford; "Earthquake Earl," they called him. To complement his straight-ahead running, they also signed a flashy halfback named Lovell Coleman. The two of them ripped western defences to shreds for the next five years. In 1961 Lunsford racked up more than a mile in rushing, 1,794 yards, to set a league record that would stand until another Stampeder back, Willie Burden, ran for 1,896 in 1975. In a 1962 Labour Day game against Edmonton, Lunsford scored 5 touchdowns. Coleman would lead the league in rushing in 1963 and 1964. The offensive line was bolstered by future Hall-of-Famer Tony Pajaczkowski at guard, the defence by linebackers Wayne Harris and John Helton. Quarterback Joe Kapp had led the West in pass attempts and yardage in 1959 and 1960. Calgary seemed to have all the ingredients. But then came another of those judgement calls.

Stampeder management was nervous about Kapp's knees and his rambling ways. So in a dramatic swap midway through the 1961 season, they had sent him to B.C. for four players and had brought in Eagle Day, a slim, hand-clapping quarterback with a quick release and a pinpoint arm. It was not one of those trades that helped both teams. Kapp took the Lions into the 1963 and 1964 Grey Cups; Day was just another adequate quarterback.

Bad luck swarmed the Stampeders like blackflies. On the last play of the last game of the 1962 western final, with the Stamps leading, their normally poised kick returner Harvey Wylie panicked and tried to soccer-kick a rolling punt out of his end zone. He whiffed on it and Winnipeg end Farrell Funston flopped on it for the winning touchdown. The Bombers, not the Stamps, went to the Grey Cup.

And on perhaps the blackest night in Stampeder football history, the team took a 26-point lead into the second game of the 1963 western final against Saskatchewan, systematically frittered it away at Taylor Field, and lost the round 48-47. That second game has been called the Miracle of Taylor Field and football coroners have been analyzing it ever since. How could a good Calgary team have collapsed so completely?

Keith Matthews was there and has a plausible theory. The former Calgary *Herald* sports editor says, "In all my years in Canada, and at sea during the war, I have never been so cold. And that was sitting in the press box. I don't know how any player could function on the field. Right after the game I caught a cab and asked the driver how cold it was. He said it had just been announced on the radio that it was eighteen below zero Fahrenheit, and with the wind figured in, the wind-chill factor was fifty-six below, Fahrenheit. At the hotel, my hands were so stiff I couldn't type, so I just dictated my story on the phone. I doubt that any football game has ever been played under such murderous conditions."

By mid-decade, the Stampeders were rebuilding again, starting with two colossal pass-catchers, Terry Evanshen and Herman Harrison. To service the two of them, the team acquired quarterback Pete Liske from Toronto. The three took the Stampeders to a first-place finish in 1967, and to more heartbreak. Evanshen, who caught a record 96 passes in the regular season, suffered a broken leg in that house of horrors, Taylor Field, and the Roughriders knocked the Stamps out of the playoffs.

Faced with the retirement of Lunsford and the decline of Coleman's talent, coach Jerry Williams had elected to live or die by the pass. It worked with the level-headed Liske, tucked securely into the pocket behind offensive linemen Lanny Boleski, Roger Kramer, Bob Leuck, Mike Spitzer and Chuck Zickefoose, throwing as many as forty times a game, often with six receivers set loose on a play. This airborne assault took the Stampeders to the 1967 Grey Cup against Ottawa. But without the threat of a running game, the Ottawa Rough Riders unloaded on Liske. He threw 2 touchdown passes and ran in a third but, as had been the case for many years, it wasn't enough. The Rough Riders, behind the improvisational, roll-out-minded Russ Jackson, won the national title 24-21.

But it all came together in 1968, twenty years after the Stampeders' last appearance in a Grey Cup game. Williams gave way to Jim Duncan that year, and Duncan took a heavy gamble. He made Jerry Keeling, his versatile three-time all-Canada all-star defensive back, his starting quarterback. Keeling was a throwback to an earlier era, when players played on both sides of the ball, but even his most ardent fans would never argue that he was a great quarterback. A great defensive back yes, but he appeared to be a career backup at quarterback until Duncan gave him his chance.

With Keeling at quarterback, everything turned around. The Stampeders went to the Grey Cup games two years in a row, just as they had under Keith Spaith in 1948 and 1949.

In 1970 Calgary squeaked into it when, in another haunted-house scenario at Taylor Field, they won on the margin of Larry Robinson's wind-challenged 32-yard field goal into the bared teeth of a blizzard. Robinson got good foot on the ball but, as it rose, the forty-mile-a-hour wind caught it, turned it and almost stopped it, until it floated through the uprights with inches to spare. The Stampeders may not have been completely defrosted a week later in Toronto. They managed only 172 yards total offence and fell to Montreal 23-10.

But a year later, in Vancouver's Empire Stadium, they won their Grey Cup, beating Toronto with a magnificent defensive effort. Keeling completed just 6 passes and threw a disastrous interception in the final minutes of the game. It was then that the Stamps got the benefit of another "Karpuk," in the shape of Leon McQuay. The Grey Cup rode to Calgary, this time by jet rather than by train.

At the end of the next season, Harris, the Grey Cup player-of-the-game, retired. Keeling moved to Ottawa and took the Rough Riders to the 1973 Grey Cup game. Liske was traded to B.C. Another cycle was starting.

It would be two decades before the Stampeders would ride into another Grey Cup, the first year under Danny Barrett, the second under Doug Flutie. But every November, a contingent of white-hatted westerners would converge on the host city. Flapjacks and chuckwagons would forevermore be part of football in Canada.

In the beginning, there was rugby football, the sport from which the game of Canadian football emerged around the turn of the last century. This team of young Vancouver worthies drew crowds of up to 3,000 spectators to its games held at the city's Hastings Park and Brockton Oval grounds in 1890–91. VANCOUVER CITY ARCHIVES

DOMINION
FOOTBALL CHAMPIONSHIP

1950   *Official Programme*   Price 25c

The Toronto Argonauts franchise was the first postwar powerhouse, fuelled exclusively by homegrown Canadian talent. The dynamic Joe Krol and Royal Copeland— the "Gold Dust Twins"—led the Argos to three consecutive Grey Cup victories in the mid-1940s.

Below: Copeland (#77) leaps to catch a pass from Krol (#55) *(inset, top left)* for the Argos' only touchdown in a tight 10–9 victory over Winnipeg in the 1947 game. By 1950, teams like the Argos had already started to base their game on imported stars, relegating Canadians like Krol and Copeland to a supporting role. CANADIAN FOOTBALL HALL OF FAME (CFHF)

Left: Many players, like Ottawa Rough Rider running back Tony Golab (#72), had their careers interrupted by the Second World War. League play was suspended in 1942 and not resumed until after VE Day. CFHF

The 1950 amalgamation of the
Hamilton Tigers and Wildcats
to form the Tiger-Cats created
the nucleus of a two-decade
winning tradition.

Above: The Ti-Cats' first coach
and general manager, Carl Voyles,
established a simple yet effective
style of play. CFHF

Right: Jake Gaudaur rose from
Ti-Cats team captain in the
early 1950s, to president and part
owner of the club in the 1960s,
and ultimately to commissioner
of the CFL. CFHF

Below: Hard-rock head coach Jim Trimble, who took over the Ti-Cats in the mid-1950s, instilled a win-at-all-costs determination in his players and took them to five Grey Cup games. CFHF

Left: A key to the Ti-Cats' success was the relentless pursuit of their hard-charging defenders. Here, guard Dave Suminski (#64) chases down Montreal's "Prince" Hal Patterson (#75), the dominant pass receiver in the Big Four throughout the 1950s. CFHF

Exuberant Calgary Stampeder fans breathed fresh Rocky Mountain air into the Grey Cup festivities in 1948. Hundreds of white-Stetsoned celebrants swept across the street from their special train at Toronto's Union Station—complete with chuckwagons and horses— transforming the normally staid Royal York Hotel into a temporary outpost of the Calgary Stampede. Their annual pancake breakfast, held that year on the steps of Toronto City Hall, became a staple of Grey Cup fare. Best of all, from a Calgary point of view, their team scored an upset victory that year over the heavily favoured Ottawa Rough Riders. CFHF; inset photo: VANCOUVER SUN

Throughout this era, the annual celebrations surrounding Canada's football championships grew into a week-long pageant. Each team's candidate vied to be Miss Grey Cup. The Grey Cup parade was a chance to poke fun at regional rivalries. Attendance at the game grew from 18,000 in 1945 to 38,000 in 1960, and millions more Canadians held Grey Cup parties in their homes, where they watched the contest on that new wonder, television.

VANCOUVER SUN

The Edmonton Eskimos were the era's first western dynasty.

Left: In the middle of this pile-up, a future premier of Alberta, Don Getty, then a quarterback of the Eskimos, drives the ball over the Montreal goal line in the 1956 Grey Cup. CANAPRESS PHOTO SERVICE

Below: Best known for his offensive abilities, the Eskimos' Jackie Parker (#91) also excelled as a defender. Here, he reaches under the arm of Montreal's Hal Patterson to deflect a pass. VANCOUVER SUN

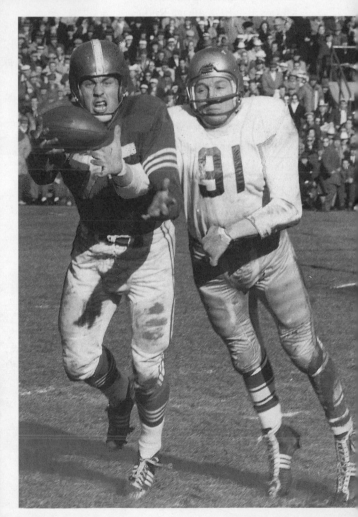

Playoff football on the prairies often meant playing through snow on frozen ground in sub-zero temperatures. CFHF

Below: One key to Edmonton's success was stability on their star-studded roster. Front row *(l–r):* End and punter Vic Chapman, tackle Ed Gray, guard Mike Kmech, centre Don Stephenson, guard Roy Stevenson, tackle Nat Dye, end Tommy Joe Coffey. Back row *(l–r):* Halfback Joe-Bob Smith, fullback Jim Shipka, quarterback Jackie Parker, fullback Normie Kwong, halfback Howie Shumm. (Absent: Fullback Johnny Bright, halfback Rollie Miles, end Jim Letcavits.) VANCOUVER SUN

Inset right: A fresh-faced Jackie Parker is still wide-eyed after his 90-yard run helped spark Edmonton's 26–25 victory over Montreal in the 1954 Grey Cup. VANCOUVER SUN

Overleaf: Ottawa's diminutive superstar, Ron Stewart (#11), climbs the back of a defender in an effort to get to the ball. CFHF

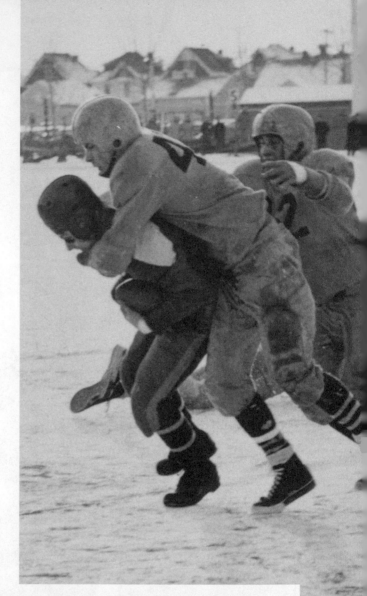

CHAPTER THREE

Ol' Spaghetti Legs:
Edmonton Eskimos

For twelve and a half years he flashed past our eyes like a blazing comet throwing off sparks of dazzling light. He wore the colours of three teams, the green and gold of the Edmonton Eskimos, the double-blue of the Toronto Argonauts and the Hallowe'en orange and black of the B.C. Lions.

But we first absorbed him from a grainy, flickering black and white image, the grey components of early television. Jackie Parker was, and remains, the man who made the Run, and he did it before what passed for a national audience in 1954.

Canadians of a certain age can still remember where they were when Parker began his run to football glory. Those who saw the game probably did so standing on the sidewalk in front of an appliance store, or gathered in the knotty-pine-panelled rec room of the only neighbour on the block who owned a television set, or in a tavern in an American border town.

Canada was not a television culture in 1954. There were radios in nine out of ten Canadian households, but television was something new and not always affordable. In 1951 there were only 60,000 sets in Canada. In 1952, when the Canadian Broadcasting Corporation launched its national television network, there were 147,000 black and white sets, retailed at an average $240, tuning in. Starting September 6, 1952, when Archbishop Paul-Émile Léger blessed the CBFT control room in Montreal (Toronto signed on two days later, featuring a promising young pianist named Glenn Gould), CBC network television consisted of three hours of daily programming reaching 26 per cent of Canada's 15 million people. Not all of them trusted the new medium. Vancouver columnist Jack Scott, writing in *Liberty* magazine in 1952, warned, "Television is the opium of home life. It can mesmerise your family all night."

By 1954, the CBC consisted of five public stations and four private stations, feeding 1.4 million home sets. There was the pressing need to supply new and important programming for this growing audience, original Canadian programming to meet the rigorous demands of the CBC's mandate. Despite the network's primary focus on news, drama and variety, sports was always a reliable and available option.

The annual Grey Cup game had been a national obsession on the prairies and in central Canada since the turn of the century. But it was a long step down in prestige from the National Hockey League and its Stanley Cup playoffs. Most Canadian sports fans became football fans for one week in November. Canadian kids did not squat in front of huge console radios on Saturday night after a macaroni and cheese dinner to listen raptly to football as they did to the tales of hockey magic spun so eloquently from the gondola above the ice at Maple Leaf Gardens by Foster Hewitt. Ironically, Hewitt had done the first Grey Cup radio broadcast in 1930, huddling in his tweed overcoat on the wind-lashed roof of Toronto's Varsity Stadium as Toronto Balmy Beach defeated the Regina Football Club 11-6 before 3,914 spectators. The experiment was successful. By 1932, most Canadian teams had their own local game broadcasts.

The CBC paid a royalty of $7,500 to televise the 1952 Grey Cup game, Toronto versus Edmonton, within the limited range of Toronto's CBLT. Two years later, the game was to go big-time, as CBC and NBC paid $350,000 for co-operative rights. The American network had lost its rights to the U.S. college game of the week and was looking to fill the Saturday afternoon sports gap.

The national print media was busy telling Canadians about a football colossus in Montreal; a passing wizard named Sam "The Rifle" Etcheverry was filling eastern skies with spiralling footballs. There were also frequent dispatches from western Canada about a man of few words and diminishing hair, Frank Ivy, who had assembled in Edmonton a powerhouse of young American rookies to go along with a complement of small but very mobile Canadian linemen.

Edmonton had been a part of Canadian football now and again since 1891 but had never won a Grey Cup. Wartime restrictions and lack of funds had forced the team to retire the franchise in 1939. They were gone ten years but came back with a drumroll and a one-man parade when Annis Stukus was hired as coach and general manager. Stukus, a superb promoter, arrived in Edmonton in March 1949 and had a team on the field by August. Operating on a $44,000 annual budget, he recruited players from the University of Alberta, including a 155-pound punt returner named Peter Lougheed, who would one day become premier of Alberta. Stukus signed a nineteen-year-old wrestler named Gene Kiniski and also persuaded eleven players from the Argonaut roster to join him, the most outrageous raid since the Fenians hit New Brunswick.

The first thing Stukus did was introduce himself to the starved football fans of Edmonton by making 92 booster speeches in 110 days. "That was my record until I went to Vancouver to run the Lions," he says. "I made 93 speeches in 100 days in Vancouver."

The second thing he did was reinstate himself as a player, something he initially had no intention of doing.

"At our second training camp, I looked at our kickers and I had guys who were kicking field goals from every angle of the field. Then I put a rush on them to see if they could kick with some mean linemen charging down their throats. Suddenly I didn't have a kicker who could get it over the line of scrimmage, let alone the crossbar. I had brought my brother Bill out to play quarterback and I asked him what we should do for a kicker. He said, 'What about you?' Well, I hadn't kicked in anger in four years, but I started running sprints to get into shape: run forty yards, sprint forty yards. When I could sprint two hundred yards, I figured I was ready."

The third thing he did was invent the wonderful wristwatch caper. The watch was a $75 Gruen Very-Thin on a leather strap. It came to have the power to drive strong men mad and added to the considerable Stukus legend.

It all began when the Montreal Alouettes came west for an exhibition game with the Calgary Stampeders, and Stukus persuaded them to play a second game against the Eskimos.

"I was running around getting the guys ready, taking care of all the details of a game arranged at the last minute. We scored early, and I went in to take the convert. I got halfway out on the field before I noticed I was still wearing my watch and a ring, so I pulled the cuffs of my sweater down as far as I could.

"In the last minute of the game, we were behind by a point and I went in to try a field goal. Then I had an inspiration. I showed the guys in the huddle my watch and said, 'Boys, you know I don't believe in fining players, but if this watch of mine gets one scratch on it, I'm fining each one of you $75.' They hold, I kick it through, we win by 2 points, and the guys carried their old playing coach off the field.

"I had another inspiration in the dressing room. I grabbed one player and said, 'See that guy over there? He's from Canadian Press. I want you to snitch on me to him. Tell him about your coach wearing his wrist-watch on the field.

"The CP guy comes and asks me about it. I say, 'I certainly wouldn't do a thing like that on purpose. It just happened in the excitement of the game. But now that you mention it, it really made my guys block on the kicks, so I may just keep wearing it.' And of course I did. It got great publicity everywhere we played. And a lot of defensive guys got twisted in knots trying to rip it off my wrist, forgetting all about trying to block the kick.

"I even invented the bounty story. I told a couple of reporters I'd heard that some coaches were offering bonus money for my watch. We went to Winnipeg, and at a pre-game rally I said, 'Cheap Winnipeg bastards. Little Regina offers $100 for my watch. Calgary bids $50. Winnipeg? A measly $25.' It drove them crazy."

Forty-two years after his last kick, Stukus says people still ask him what happened to the watch. Is it in the Canadian Football Hall of Fame? "When [my wife] Doris and I left Edmonton and moved back to Toronto, our daughter was teaching elementary school," he says. "She said the kids wanted to see my famous watch. So I let her take it. By the time it had passed around the room, all I got back was half the strap and the casing. That watch survived thirty-nine football games without even a scratch on the crystal. But it couldn't survive a roomful of school kids."

Stukus had some success in Edmonton, improving the Esks from 4-10 in his first year to 8-6 in his third and last, and he built a solid foundation before handing his cap and whistle over to playing-coach Frank Filchock and heading back to the newspaper business in Toronto. When Filchock too failed to bring home a championship, losing the Grey Cup 21-11 to the Argos in Toronto, he was replaced by Darrell Royal in 1953. Royal came to the Eskimos from the University of Oklahoma, where he had been an assistant under legendary Sooners head coach Bud Wilkinson, innovator of a little wrinkle in offensive alignment that came to define the demarcation between modern and old-fashioned football strategy. It was known as the "split-T."

At the time, most teams employed a straightforward T formation in which offensive linemen crouched shoulder to shoulder, thrusting forward to power defenders aside and create holes for the running backs by main strength alone. In the split-T formation, with the offensive linemen spaced four feet apart rather than in the traditional phalanx, defences had to spread accordingly. This allowed the Edmonton running backs to shoot the gaps, as their linemen had only to tie up their opponents momentarily rather than move mountains of meat and muscle out of the way.

Royal's strategy brought regular-season success, as the Esks went 12-4 and finished first in the West. Rookie Billy Vessels ran for 924 yards and was named the first recipient of the Schenley Award as the nation's outstanding player of the year in 1953. But the team lost to the Winnipeg Blue Bombers in the best-of-three final. Vessels suffered serious injuries and would never again play for Edmonton; Royal, too, would not return.

Ivy, Parker and the good times arrived in 1954. Ivy, tall and bald enough to deserve the nickname "Pop," inherited a team that had benefited from a season's adjustment to the new system. In order to be most effective, the speed-based split-T required a quarterback. Ivy had just such a man in twenty-one-year-old Bernie Faloney. Faloney had been all-American at the University of Maryland. He had a good arm and the hands of a pickpocket. The Eskimo running game used quick brush blocks, motion and Faloney's brilliant ball-faking.

Right from the start, Ivy had an enviable problem. He had two superb fullbacks, both of them acquired from Calgary. One was Normie Kwong, known as "the China Clipper." Normie, born Kwong Lim in Calgary, had gone against his mother's wishes and pursued a football career that now netted him $10,000 a year, including bonuses. He was a chunky, near-sighted, straight-ahead runner who ran almost horizontally, knifing low into scrimmage pile-ups, disappearing momentarily and then popping out corklike with consistent gains. Kwong routinely carried the ball twenty-five times a game. But his faking was so effective that he was routinely tackled forty times a game.

Johnny Bright, an all-American from Drake University, was a massive physical specimen, hugely muscled, with eyebrows like a set of hairbrushes. He was an unsubtle basher. While at Drake, Bright had become a national celebrity. Wilbanks Smith, an enemy lineman, had been photographed throwing a vicious forearm that smashed Bright's jaw. The picture made the cover of *Life* magazine. Away from football, Bright was a high school English teacher, encouraging youngsters to appreciate the power of words over physical strength. Bright had injured both shoulders while playing linebacker with Calgary. Edmonton got him off the discard rack for $350.

Ivy solved his dilemma shrewdly, in a way that seemed bizarre at first. If you have two qualified fullbacks, he thought, don't cut one; find a way to use both. And so was born the twin-fullback formation. Kwong infiltrated enemy lines, Bright bombarded them. Halfbacks Parker,

Rollie Miles and Earl Lindley, all three as versatile as Swiss Army knives, ran sweeps, counter plays and pass routes. Bright and Kwong would go on to take turns leading the league in rushing, racking up more than a 1,000 yards *each* in two seasons, 1957 and 1958.

Ivy was one of the great innovative geniuses of Canadian football. Eagle Keys, Ivy's sturdy offensive centre—Keys broke in with Montreal and was an all-star in both divisions—and later a member of his coaching staff, is unequivocal in his praise of Ivy. "You have to look at his success in terms of the time. When he coached Edmonton he had one assistant coach, so he had to know offence and defence. He had to coach, not just delegate to a pile of assistants. There was no exchange of game film and no playbooks. He did it on the blackboard. He got along well with his players, and when he left to go south, he was a winner there, too. He was a great coach."

Peahead Walker was as enamoured with the pass as Pop Ivy was with the run.

Alouette coach Douglas "Peahead" Walker was a plump, drawling southerner who was as enamoured with the pass as Ivy was with the run. Small wonder. Walker had Sam Etcheverry at quarterback and superb receivers like Hal Patterson and Red O'Quinn in addition to backs like Joey Pal, Pat Abbruzzi, Bill Bewley, Alex Webster and Chuck Hunsinger, all of whom could run and catch. Those assets were coupled with huge linemen like Tex Coulter, guard-tackle Herbie Trawick, a seven-time all-star, and Jim Staton.

And so these two powerful tides, west and east, met at the football confluence, Toronto's Varsity Stadium, on November 27, 1954. A crowd of 27,321 packed the stadium on a clear, cold day. One fan, employed by a local retailer to stroll along Bloor Street on a pair of stilts, dressed as Santa and bearing a sandwich board advertising the store, propped himself up against the outside of the fence and enjoyed a free view of the day's proceedings. At that time, Canadian professional football games were not regularly televised, and there was no interlocking schedule in the two divisions; consequently, fans didn't know enough about each other's teams to establish reasonable betting form. That may have accounted for Montreal being established as the overwhelming 6-1 favourite at the start of Grey Cup week. But the odds dropped to 3-1 as more and more Albertans arrived in Toronto, bearing "Love Those Esks" buttons on their western-cut lapels and prairie dollars in their pockets.

The post-game statistics would indicate overwhelmingly that the bookies were dead on when they put their faith in Etcheverry's passing arm. The Rifle had one of the greatest Grey Cup games in history, throwing 3 touchdown passes and generating an awesome 698 yards in total offence. O'Quinn was extraordinary, catching 13 passes for 316 yards and 2 touchdowns and running 93 yards for a third. The Esks had 567 yards in total offence as the viewing nation learned that the days of conventional, run-based football were gone; free-wheeling football had arrived. But despite Etcheverry and O'Quinn, Montreal lost that game. They lost it to defence and a monumental boner.

Montreal seemed comfortably ahead in the second half, with a 25-14 lead. But strange things began to happen. Rollie Miles had started the game with three cracked ribs and was having trouble breathing. Ivy replaced him with an obscure backup running back. Faloney remembers, "I called a sweep to Glenn Lipmann. He was in for Miles and he went 35 yards for a touchdown. It was tight going but we put it together in the fourth quarter."

Lipmann's converted touchdown made it 25-20 (touchdowns were worth 5 points in 1954), but with the clock running down, Montreal was still ahead and looking for the kill. With three and a half minutes left, they moved to Edmonton's 10-yard line. Smelling blood, Etcheverry called a sweep to the left, pitching the ball deep and wide to Hunsinger. At the line of scrimmage, Hunsinger was met and sandwiched by Rollie Prather and Ted Tully and forgot every rule of possession he had ever learned—he pitched the ball out wildly to a phantom teammate. The ball bounced. On the run, defensive halfback Parker bent low and fielded it on a short hop, like the baseball player he had also been. Then Parker began to run towards a Montreal goal-line he couldn't see through his weary eyes. Desperately, Etcheverry set out in pursuit. Bright, also playing defensive half, moved step-by-step with Parker, conscious that if he threw a block on Etcheverry he would nullify the play. Parker went 90 yards. Someone who must have timed it claims Parker ran for fifteen seconds, long enough to make permanent history. He collapsed in a heaving heap in the end zone. It was 25-25. The convert won it for the West.

There is one of those clinging legends that the Edmonton centre, Eagle Keys, who had suffered a hairline fracture of his lower leg earlier in the game, hobbled gamely out to snap the ball for the convert. Not true. Backup Bill Briggs snapped it; Bob Dean, another ex-Maryland Terrapin, who hadn't missed a convert all year, booted it through. The Eskimos were the champions, and reverberations of that game are still ringing.

Poor Hunsinger never played for Montreal again. In the off-season, sympathetic Montreal fans bombarded him with hundreds of "Cheer Up, Chuck" cards. He attended the 1955 training camp but was an early cut. Coach Walker said of the lethal giveaway, "The boy got a brainstorm. He just threw it away."

But it was the sage of Canadian sportswriters, Jim Coleman, who had covered his first Grey Cup game in 1931, who pointed out the original sin. He wrote, "The Alouettes got too greedy. They elected to go for another touchdown rather than settling for an almost-certain field goal that would have put the game beyond doubt."

In retrospect, Etcheverry says today, "Maybe I should have tried for a field goal or a single point. But all I knew was that we had a great team that year. I didn't get any signal from the bench to kick and I didn't expect it. I think everybody in the park knew we were going for another touchdown."

The game established some heavy points: (1) Statistics are for mathematicians. (2) Television and football were born for each other. (3) You did not have to play for the Toronto Maple Leafs to become a national hero. An alien from Tennessee could qualify.

Four decades later, in his winter home in Palm Desert, California, where he plays golf and sips his Beefeater's, Parker could savour the day if not the consequences. "I don't remember much about the play and the run, except that I was so damned tired and so sore. You have to remember that we played twenty-seven games that season. The Grey Cup game was the twenty-seventh and we were all pretty banged up. Most of us played both ways, sixty minutes a game. I had a bad leg, Rollie had broken ribs, everybody was hurtin'. When I fell into the end zone, at that moment, it just meant that we were ahead, maybe the season was over. But I didn't think the play was anything special, that people would remember it. It was after that it was built up to much. But honest, I don't remember much about the run except being so tired. A day later, I felt good about it for the young Canadians and the older vets on the team. It meant the world to them. It took longer to settle in on me."

Jack Dickerson Parker was born in East Tennessee. Even as a twenty-one-year-old Edmonton rookie, he had the look of a boy who should be walking out of a pine copse, a rifle in one hand, a brace of possums in the other. He had Bing Crosby ears, high cheekbones that framed startling blue eyes and gold teeth that winked out of his smile. His wavy hair was the colour of bleached straw. His hands were enormous, like bunches of bananas on his long arms. His shoulders were wide. His poor legs were sticks.

Parker's boyhood was filled with baseball, happiness and hazards.

"We lived in Knoxville and I split my time between our own home and my grandmother's home a few blocks away," he recalls. "We were healthy kids because we were playing outside all the time. I always had a baseball mitt because I was going to be a baseball player, play for the Yankees. But the worst thing that ever happened, worse than my appendix blowing up when I was about twelve, was falling into the Tennessee River when I was thirteen. We were fishing for carp and I fell in behind the East Tennessee Packing Plant, where the water was full of blood and fish guts. We either ran barefoot or wore cheap running shoes and we all had athlete's foot. Well, I got a terrible infection in my left foot. For a while they were talking seriously about amputating it.

"The pain was awful and I was really scared. Lucky for me, they had just developed penicillin. Every second day, I had to go to my doctor. He'd give me an injection and then he'd take a scalpel and ream out the holes where the pus was and cut away the dead meat. I was on crutches for six months, but they saved the foot."

Football was not part of Parker's life then, just baseball. "I didn't play high school football until my senior year. My baseball coach was the school's football coach. He asked me to come out as the punter and backup running back. When I went on to Jones County Junior College, I was the third-string tailback until the first two got hurt. Jones was a great little school. I got a half-scholarship and paid $27 a month for room, board, tuition and a damn fine education. Sure, there was a lot of rice, potatoes and field peas on the table, but it was a fine school."

Parker was seventeen when he fell in love with, and married, a softball player named Peggy Jo Pease. Parker was offered a baseball scholarship at Mississippi State, but it was blocked because the Southeast Conference did not give scholarships to married athletes. No problem. The Parkers got a divorce of convenience, Parker got the scholarship and he and Peggy Jo remarried six months later. Mississippi got a football player and a scholar. In the final semester of his senior year, Parker made the Dean's List in the education faculty and was a President's Scholar with five As and a B.

Parker was a four-year football sensation at MSU, but he still planned to turn pro as a baseball player. He didn't think he was a good enough football player. Darrell Royal did, though. The American coach had put in a year as the Esks' coach before taking over at MSU. He convinced Parker to give it a try at Edmonton, which brought him to Canada in time for the 1954 season. Even after that, Parker wasn't convinced.

"I liked Edmonton, but after that first season, I was all beat up and down to 175 pounds. I went back to Knoxville and sold cars, did pretty good at it. The football Yankees invited me to New York. I went up there. I liked the team, but I just couldn't see myself living in a city that big. The Eskimos were asking me to come back, Wellington Mara of the Giants wanted me, so I decided that maybe I could get a career out of football. We went back to Edmonton and bought a house and settled in."

Edmonton broadcaster Bryan Hall met Parker when they were both rookies in their professions, and Hall became Parker's Boswell, habitually opening interviews with other media people with the question, "Don't you think Jackie Parker is the greatest player who ever lived?" He has not changed his pitch.

"I got into radio in 1954, covering the Eskimos. I remember when this curly-haired guy with the big ears and the quiet demeanour reported to camp. He was from the start, and he was as long as I've known him, the greatest, smartest, luckiest athlete I've ever seen. He has never changed. He'll beat you at golf, at curling, at Hollywood gin. Whatever it is, he'll beat your ass. I remember watching the World Series with him. He'd say, 'Now Bryan, watch that runner on second. He's figured out the pitcher's motion and he's going to steal on the next pitch.' And it would happen.

"He was good, he was lucky, things happened for him. I think he won three cars in three draws at sports banquets he used to attend. I saw him one day win a game by kicking two field goals. Both kicks hit the crossbar and rolled up and over. His teammates loved him; they always knew he'd figure out a way to win. Those Labour Day games against Calgary, the guys would go to Jack's house, play cards all night, report for pre-game breakfast and then Jack would go out and throw 2 or 3 touchdown passes."

Norm Fieldgate, who played 223 games at linebacker for the B.C. Lions from 1954 to 1967, offers the defensive player's perspective. "Jackie did so many things, played so many positions. It was always a bit of a relief when he played halfback or flanker because he wasn't handling the ball on every play. I remember after one game when the Eskimos had really beaten us up, I was in the dressing room, smiling. Someone asked me why I was smiling. I said, 'I had a good day today, I touched Parker once.'

Eskimos general manager Joe Ryan said he'd be happy to trade Parker— for $50,000 and 24 Canadian players.

"Playing all those positions, offence and defence, he had to have great instincts, because they couldn't coach him in all those positions. He had to do it all from reaction.

"He looked like a rack of bones, but I could never believe the shock you got when you tackled him. He was deceptively fast, he'd get those legs of his going in different directions. And he was tough. I don't think he sat out many games in his career."

Ted Tully, the great Edmonton linebacker who came to the Eskimos straight from the Vancouver junior football ranks, says today, "I swear to

God Jackie had a seventh sense when it came to finding a way to win a football game. He was the most competitive man I ever saw. If he was playing golf with Arnold Palmer, I'd put my money on Jackie. One year Jackie talked Matt Baldwin into letting Jackie curl with him, even though he'd never thrown a stone. In no time he was one of the finest seconds in Alberta. I've never seen him fail at anything. What do you do with a guy who can do anything and do it better than anyone else?"

Competitive? Vancouver writer Jim Taylor recalls sitting with Parker on an airliner when they were served lunch. Parker looked at his plate and said, "I bet there's between 124 and 133 peas in that pile." Taylor, not a big spender, covered the bet for a buck and they actually counted the peas. There were 129. Parker tucked away Taylor's buck and explained that a guy who worked in the kitchen of a Knoxville hotel had told him the average restaurant scoop of peas always worked out to between 124 and 133.

Valuable? Eskimo general manager Joe Ryan once said he would be happy to trade Parker. "For $50,000 and twenty-four Canadian players."

Adored? Edmonton media relations director Allen Watt said, "Jackie would have made an excellent Pope. He has that aura about him."

Parker led the Eskimos to Grey Cup championships in the next two seasons as well. In 1955, the Eskimos again faced the Alouettes, this time in Vancouver, the first time the final had been played in western Canada; the first time, in fact, that the game had taken place anywhere but Toronto in more than a decade. Ivy, aware of the distractions that Grey Cup week in a big town can cause, took his team to Victoria and lodged them in the austere Empress Hotel. Four thousand Victorians turned out one afternoon to watch the team practise at Royal Athletic Park. At first, the blue-rinse dowagers and retired Raj majors who took tea, crumpets and cucumber sandwiches in the lobby of the Empress every afternoon to the strains of Billy Tickle's string quartet were intimidated by the Edmonton players as they headed for practice in their sweats, carrying their cleats in their hands. But by mid-week they were calling out, "Mr. Bright, do sign my doily," and, "Don't be too hard on them, Mr. Ivy, they're lovely boys."

Special trains from across the country converged on the rainy west-coast city in the days before the game. One brought 230 members of the

Toronto Junior Board of Trade, who were somewhat dismayed, in the cavalcade of floats that made up the Grey Cup parade, to see four dedicated to the host city's vision of "Toronto the Good": one depicting the famed Royal York Hotel as a bordello draped in red lights and mattresses; another graced with a scantily covered artist's model to represent the height of Toronto culture; a third showing Bay Street stockbrokers in the company of pawnbrokers and loan sharks; a fourth featuring one of Toronto's brand spanking new subway trains descending through a sewer grating. So much for the festival of national goodwill.

Grounds crews had ministered to the soggy Empire Stadium turf, laying down nine tons of straw in the week before the game to soak up excess moisture. A nylon tarpaulin lay at hand in case further rains threatened. By far the largest ever Grey Cup crowd—more than 39,000 paid attendance—filled the arena built to host the previous year's British Empire Games.

Parker started the game at quarterback, his rise to prominence the previous season having allowed Ivy to sleep easier when Bernie Faloney, nursing a chronic knee injury, opted for an assistant coaching job offered by the Calgary Stampeders. To replace Eagle Keys at centre, whose own leg injury had led him to settle for a scouting post with the Eskimos, Ivy had brought in another Sooner, all-American Kurt Burris, who shored up the blocking in front of Parker.

Eastern pundits sought comfort in the fact that the Eskimos had won the previous year on what many considered a fluke play. They made the Alouettes odds-on favourites. In the first half, it looked as if their prediction would come true, as Edmonton trailed Montreal 19-18 after two quarters of play.

But the Eskimos stuck to their game plan, grinding it out along the ground. Kwong carried 29 times for 135 yards and 2 touchdowns. Bright took the ball 8 times for 90 yards and knocked Montreal defender J.C. Caroline senseless driving for the goal-line. Rollie Miles gained 73 yards on only 5 carries, and Earl Lindley ran 6 times for 45 yards. And then there was Parker. Apart from directing the overwhelming Edmonton offence, he also starred on defence, intercepting 1 pass and making a Grey Cup–record 29 tackles. He swarmed all over the field for fifty-three minutes that day, standing at the sidelines only for kicking plays and the final minutes, when, the game well in hand, Ivy subbed Don Getty at quarterback. The Eskimos won it 34-19.

Euphoric Eskimo fans flooded into the end zone in the game's final seconds, causing referee Paul Dojack to call a halt. They streamed out of the stadium, some singing, to the tune celebrating Davy Crockett, another Tennessee legend, "Jackie, Jackie Parker. King of the old split-T!"

Still stoked with competitive fire after the game, Parker spoke bluntly. "We beat 'em in the second half," he told a circle of reporters. "Hell, we just beat 'em to death. Anyway, them Alouettes can't say we lucked out on 'em this year." Coach Ivy stood in awe of his quarterback's desire: "Jackie's got a burning will to win, but he hides it, casual-like. He keeps the pressure on because he has fire inside. Parker's physical ability is no better than average . . . but it's the tiger in him that makes him great."

In 1956, the wily Ivy experimented again. In early November, he elevated University of Western Ontario graduate Don Getty from backup to starting quarterback, freeing Parker up as a running back. Getty, whom Pop Ivy called "the best Canadian-born passer I've ever seen," was superb in the western playoffs, and Ivy gave him the start in the Grey Cup game. It was held once more in Toronto, not far from the scene of Getty's triumphs as a Western Mustang. In front of him was a young, rebuilt line featuring tackle Roger Nelson, another of the growing Oklahoma horde, who had returned after sitting out the 1955 season to study dentistry; rookie end Bill Walker, another Maryland Terrapin all-American; veteran end and still another transplanted Oklahoman Frankie Anderson; and rookie centre Johnny Tatum, stepping into Kurt Burris's cleats straight from the University of Texas Longhorns. It did not seem to matter who Eskimo coaches put in front of their all-star backfield, they never failed to hold the opposition at bay. Normie Kwong had run for a personal-best 1,437 yards and a 6.2 yard average in regular season play. Yet, incredibly, odds-makers favoured Montreal for the third straight year.

The teams held close through the first half. In the third quarter, Montreal and Edmonton were tied 20-20. Then Edmonton's long fuse ignited, and the Eskimos exploded for another 30 points to beat Montreal for the third straight time, 50-27, making this the highest-scoring Grey

Cup game yet. Parker scored 3 touchdowns and kicked a single. Getty and Bright scored 2 touchdowns each. Combined, Edmonton backs ran up 459 yards against Montreal along the ground. The final score would have been a point higher but they ran out of footballs—eighteen had been kicked into the stands—and the Esks never did convert their final touchdown. It would have been redundant.

Getty did not exactly burn up the turf, completing only 7 of 15 passes for 103 yards, but he kept his cool as he stage-managed the Eskimos' dramatic, second-half spectacular with an authority belying his relative inexperience. Wisecracking Normie Kwong had quipped before the match, "Getty, you lose this game for us and I'll cut off your supply of opium!"

After that third straight Grey Cup win, Edmonton football fans surely felt that Pop Ivy was Moses revisiting, Jackie Parker was the greatest thing to hit Alberta since Leduc #1 came in, and the Eskimos were an empire that would span decades. But the team ran into a blue wall in 1957.

The Esks piled up a superb 14-2 season that year, but they did not get past the playoffs, losing to Winnipeg in a western final that was as remarkable as any string of games the Eskimos had won. The Bombers were under a new, but very familiar, rookie head coach. Bud Grant, their great end, had been elevated directly from the playing ranks to the head coach's job with no period of apprenticeship. Winnipeg finished 12-4, beat Calgary in a rigorous semi-final and then eliminated Edmonton in a three-gamer that, in terms of points scored, was redolent of baseball. Bombers shocked Edmonton 19-7 in the first game, thanks principally to an early kickoff return touchdown by Gerry James that made Winnipeg believe in themselves.

The second game was 5-4, Edmonton, neither team crossing a goal-line. The third was tied at 2-2 at the end of regulation time, James booting the tying point in the final minute. In overtime, on a rock-hard field, Rollie Miles fumbled at punt. The ball rolled into the Edmonton end zone, Gerry Vincent gleefully grounded it for a touchdown, and Winnipeg salvaged a 17-2 victory. The Edmonton reign was over, and the Bomber reign was starting.

Edmonton couldn't regain their mastery through the rest of the 1950s. Ivy left in 1958 to coach in the National Football League, and he was replaced by a short-termer named Sam Lyle for one year before Eagle Keys took over for a span of five seasons. Reality would be harsh in the years to come.

Every year of the 1950s, Edmonton had reached at least the western finals. They had appeared in four Grey Cups and won three. To start the new decade, the Eskimos, under Parker, rallied for one last hurrah, upsetting the high-flying Blue Bombers in a low-scoring western final before bowing out 16-6 to Ottawa in the Grey Cup. From then on they began a slow, spiralling descent from which they would not emerge for the balance of the 1960s. Kwong, after thirteen years with Calgary and Edmonton, hung it up in 1960. Bright, his skills diminishing, stayed on a few more years, but his string of five straight 1,000-yard-plus seasons was over by 1961.

At the end of the 1963 season, the Eskimos, at 2-14, had the worst record in Canada. Edmonton directors, aware that they had an aging, beat-up football team with no great talent in the wings, did the unthinkable: they traded Parker. They traded him to Toronto for five players— Bill Mitchell, Joe Hernandez, Jon Rechner, Zeke Smith and Mike Wiklum—and $15,000 in cash that must have seemed like Judas dollars to Parker's fans. Parker put a good face on it, saying the usual things about there being a time to move on, pledging allegiance to his new team: "I don't think it's healthy to stay in one place too long. I've always told the Eskimos that if they could benefit by trading or selling me, I'd go along with them. I think I have four or five good years left in me and after that, I want to get into coaching." But it was a sorry day for Canadian football. The deal seemed to carry a two-way curse; Edmonton won only two games that season, Toronto three.

Parker, hurting physically and surrounded by nondescript talent in Toronto, played out the string for three years. There were flashes of his inborn talent, but it was seldom sustained. He and his knees were too old, too used up. In the summer of 1966 his name was discreetly placed on the CFL retired list. Years later, when the pain had faded, Parker could look back at his three years in Toronto as the time of his greatest humiliation, his greatest failure, and it had nothing to do with football.

Parker's brother, Fred, was a part-time journalist and full-time promoter who coattailed on Jackie's fame. One time in Toronto Fred asked his brother if he would record a jingle for the Easter Seal campaign. Parker went through some songbooks and picked out two selections, "Sentimental Journey" and "Walking the Floor over You." As requested, he went to the CBC radio studios, and once there he got a shock.

"I figured I could muddle through it if there was no one there looking at me. Well, I walk into the studio and, my God! There's a twenty-five-piece orchestra. Trombones, violins, trumpets! Right away I knew I had been conned. It turned out they were recording a network radio show and I was going to be heard from coast to coast. I was goin' to tear Fred's arm off and beat him to death with it, but he slipped out a side door. Well, it was awful. Just awful. I got the fastest sore throat in history. I couldn't hit the high notes in 'Sentimental Journey.' 'Walking the Floor' was better, but not much. Ever since I've been trying to forget that day and buy up every copy of the transcription."

By 1975, when a panel of Canadian football writers endorsed him as the greatest player of the previous twenty-five years, Parker had scored 750 career points. He had run and caught for 88 touchdowns, passed for another 88, kicked 40 field goals, 103 converts and 19 singles. He had played on three Grey Cup winners, won three Schenley Awards and seven Jeff Nicklin Awards, and been an all-star selection eight straight times.

But before that reckoning Parker would play again, briefly and unhappily, and add a few more digits to his already astonishing career numbers. In 1968, he joined the B.C. Lions as an assistant coach. And it was an indication of the sorry state of the B.C. franchise that year that midway through the season, with quarterbacks falling and failing all over the lot, Parker was asked by head coach Jim Champion to crank it one more time. He was thirty-six years old, he hadn't played a down of football in three years, and he still had those abused knees. But when he was asked to suit up, he agreed. It was a bad idea. Parker played in eight games. The Lions won one of them, tied one, lost six. Parker took a brutal pounding. He carried the ball 29 times for 67 yards, scored 1 touchdown, completed 54 passes, had 5 interceptions.

Yet Vancouver writer Jim Taylor saw nobility in that futility. Parker, he wrote, "got by on short passes and guile, trickery and deceit. The kids on the team would straggle into the dressing-room and look at him, bruised and bone-weary and naked in front of his cubicle, head down, too tired even to shower, and they'd shake their heads and whisper to each other, 'Migawd, can you imagine what he must have been like before?' "

December 14, 1983, was the best of days and the worst of days for Edmonton football. On that mid-season day, at a snap press conference, Jackie Parker was reintroduced to the Edmonton media as the new head coach of the Eskimos, with a two-year contract. The bottom had dropped out of another Edmonton dynasty the previous year, when the sainted Hugh Campbell had left to join the new United States Football League after leading the Eskimos to a stunning five Grey Cup victories in six seasons. Parker's return was a joyous thing; the Eskimos were in a state of revolt, with knives in their teeth, over the coaching of Campbell's successor. It was assumed, as it always had been, that Jackie would think of something.

But earlier that day Johnny Bright had died at age fifty-three of a massive heart attack during surgery to repair an old football injury. His death draped a pall over what ought to have been a joyous event. Choked, Parker uttered a few words in appreciation of his old comrade. Wiping away tears of grief, he said of his new job, "It's something I've always wanted to do. I've wanted to coach the Eskimos since I was a player here."

Parker was home.

CHAPTER FOUR

A Matter of Discipline:
Montreal Alouettes

On November 9, 1960, days after the Montreal Alouettes were elimi-nated from playoff contention, team owner Ted Workman did the unforgivable: he agreed to a trade that would send quarterback Sam "The Rifle" Etcheverry, who had led the Alouettes to three mid-fifties Grey Cup games, and the Alouettes' most reliable receiver, Hal Patter-son, to the Hamilton Tiger-Cats.

Etcheverry, in Ottawa on business, heard the news from his wife over the telephone. Following the team's embarrassing 30-14 loss in the Big Four sudden death playoff the preceding Saturday, he had openly con-tradicted his coach. Facing questions from reporters as to why the Als had not thrown a single pass during the first half of the game, Perry Moss had indicated that Etcheverry had a sore shoulder. Etcheverry denied it, saying that his throwing ability had been unimpaired and pointing his finger at Moss as the culprit in the questionable play selection.

Sam had also had a recent run-in with Ted Workman, young scion of a wealthy Quebec garment industry family, who had purchased controlling interest of the team in 1956. Workman, a zealot, had been pestering Etcheverry all season long to join a fundamentalist group called Moral Re-Armament. Etcheverry had finally had enough, and he told the owner in no uncertain terms that he had absolutely no interest in having his morals re-armed. Since then, Workman's enthusiasm for his star pivot had cooled noticeably.

Moral Re-Armament was an international religious and charitable movement founded in 1938 by American clergyman Frank Nathan Daniel Buchman. The movement's objective was "To restore God to leadership in the life of nations, and to work for the strengthening of morale within a country and so build a healthful national life." As admirable as that plan might have been, it is doubtful that the Reverend Buchman ever intended that Moral Re-Armament be used as a game plan for a professional football team. But exactly that happened to the Montreal Alouettes in the 1960s, and it was a presence, if not a dominating factor, in shattering a successful franchise.

Patterson, who was making his way back to his off-season home in Larned, Kansas, could not be reached right away. A few weeks earlier he had sulked off the practice field after a confrontation with Moss. Moss consistently refused to play Patterson on defence, using him on offence only. Patterson, a proud two-way player who loved to give as well as he got in the hitting department, had finally protested.

A call from Hamilton general manager Jake Gaudaur came at a time when Workman was tired of losing and fed up with what he perceived as the petulance of his veteran stars. Gaudaur had a proposal. He and ten partners had just purchased the Tiger-Cat franchise from the city and were looking to improve it. Gaudaur inquired about Etcheverry's availability. Workman said he could have him, and he would throw in Patterson, too. Gaudaur could scarcely believe his good fortune. He hastened to Montreal to complete the trade details before Workman might have second thoughts: Etcheverry for Hamilton quarterback Bernie

Faloney; Patterson for Don Paquette, a Canadian end modestly lacking in star quality.

When the papers bearing the story hit the street, Montreal went berserk in two languages. Moss, who had not been consulted but was in favour of the move, was hung in effigy from many a lamppost along Rue Ste-Catherine. As the team management's public face, he bore the brunt of the fans' wrath. Irate callers deluged the Als' head office, threatening to cancel their season tickets if the deal was allowed to go through. The team received more than one bomb threat, and two passionate pro-Etcheverry fans sent a hangman's noose to the Montreal *Gazette*, along with a note that read, "Would you be kind enough to pass this forward to Mr. Moss? Also, please give him any help he may require in putting it to use. Thanks."

Hamilton coach Jim Trimble called the proposed trade "a great one for us," then added, for propriety's sake, "and for Canadian football." Former Als great Tex Coulter, a teammate of Etcheverry and Patterson on the all-star Montreal teams of the mid-1950s, expressed a differing opinion: "For some immature rookie coach like Moss to come up here with his Boy Scout troops and mess it up is incredible. It's absolutely amazing." Herb Capozzi, who played four seasons for the Alouettes in the 1950s before becoming the B.C. Lions general manager in 1957, recalls that he had always liked and respected Workman, but "The trade was nuts. Sam was a fiery competitor and a great team leader. We always knew if he threw up before a game, we'd win it. I'll never understand the trade. It devastated the team, it devastated the attendance."

The Als' head coach was defiant: "As long as I'm the boss," declared Moss, "I will make changes that I feel will strengthen our team, and I won't be satisfied until we're in the Grey Cup." And he sprayed gasoline on the gathering flames by denigrating Etcheverry in comparison with Faloney. "It's a case of trading a great individual star for a great team star. There is no way to compare the two players insofar as records are concerned. Sam is off by himself because he is an individual star. However, the other fellow has been with only one losing team in his entire career. We feel he is the type of player we need to produce a winner."

No one will ever know whether Moss's judgement was accurate. Etcheverry, peeved at having been kept in the dark and feeling that his past heroics were unappreciated, declared that the trade had invalidated his contract with the Als, on which there was one year remaining, and skipped to St. Louis, Missouri, and the Cardinals of the National Football League to play under former Edmonton Eskimo coach Pop Ivy. The Als had lost their star quarterback, with nothing to show in return. Faloney stayed on to lead the Ti-Cats to glory. In the following 1961 season, the Als slipped to the depths of the East, not to resurface for more than a decade.

Truth be told, the team had been on the decline for some years. Since its last Grey Cup appearance in 1956, it had finished above .500 in regular season play only once. The Alouettes finished the 1960 season 5-9. Offensive production had tailed off, and their 458 points against was a league high and a franchise record. So Workman and Moss were not motivated by pique alone. And much as they idolized their Rifle and his pal Hal, Montreal fans, too, were growing increasingly sour. The crowds were dwindling at Delormier Downs, the stadium which a few years earlier had seen Jackie Robinson's historic breaking of major league baseball's colour barrier with the Montreal Royals, a Brooklyn Dodgers farm team.

Football, amateur and professional, had been played inside the ivy-covered cloister of McGill University since the inception of the Canadian game in 1881. Teams with names like the Winged Wheelers, the Cubs, the Indians and the Hornets had entertained fans with varying success until the Alouettes were formed in 1946 under the shrewd leadership of Lew Hayman, Eric Cradock, Leo Dandurand and Joe Ryan.

But the rot of disinterest was setting in by 1960. The team's last, and so far only, Grey Cup win had come more than a decade earlier, in 1949. Humbled by the upstart Calgary Stampeders in the 1948 Grey Cup, Montreal head coach Lew Hayman had enticed Tiger star Frank Filchock away from Hamilton with an offer of a two-year, $20,000 contract, use of an apartment and the loan of a late-model convertible. These inducements had paid off handsomely come Grey Cup time, in a rematch against the defending champions.

Old rivalries spiced the 1949 Montreal-Calgary match-up. Filchock had played against Stampeder head coach Les Lear during the latter's NFL playing career. Montreal's backup quarterback and kicker Ches McCance had reputedly faced Lear in less regulated battles as members of rival youth gangs in Winnipeg before both channelled their aggression between the sidelines.

The returning members of the Alouette squad had not forgotten the previous year's surprise defeat, and they overpowered Calgary in the clinches. Filchock, masterfully slithering his way around the slush-covered turf of Toronto's Varsity Stadium, set up fullback Virgil Wagner for two short dives into the end zone and lofted a 30-yard bomb to Bob Cunningham for a third touchdown. Playing on the other side of the ball, Filchock picked off 3 passes by Calgary quarterback Keith Spaith, running one back 70 yards. The Alouettes won 28-15.

Ted Reeve, the Toronto sportswriter and former Balmy Beach star, immortalized Spaith's problems in a witty bit of doggerel:

> In the quarterback passing of Spaith,
> The Westerners put all their faith,
> But the Montreal ends,
> Were not acting like friends,
> And they rushed him all over the plaith.

Filchock, a former New York Giant, had ventured north while under suspension relating to an attempt to bribe him and Giant teammate Merle Hapes to throw the 1946 NFL championship game against the Chicago Bears. A zealous New York district attorney named Frank Hogan was tipped that a two-bit gambler named Alvin Paris had offered the bribes, which the players had turned down but neglected to report. With the suspension lifted by NFL commissioner Bert Bell in July of 1950, Filchock decide to test the waters south of the border, signing with the Baltimore Colts. But those waters proved turgid, and a year later he was back in Canada, leading the Eskimos to the 1952 Grey Cup as head coach.

In the meantime, Hayman and Alouette president Leo Dandurand faced starting over. Neither was a stranger to what it took to build a winning team. Hayman had taken Toronto teams to Grey Cup victory four times in the 1930s and 1940s. Dandurand, who had tasted Stanley Cup success many times with the Montreal Canadiens hockey dynasty, had run the Alouettes from his favourite table in the Café Martin in midtown

Montreal. But neither had any interest in the task of rebuilding. They had achieved what they set out to—a national football championship for Montreal—and they decided to sell their majority interest and move on.

The new owners, local businessmen Charlie Stone, Fred Skelcher and Roy Robertson, were aware they lacked the expertise to guide a winning franchise. They knew they had a nucleus of talented players, but they needed a leader on the field and on the sidelines, someone like Filchock or Hayman. They needed a head coach, and they found him in former Wake Forest University field boss Douglas "Peahead" Walker. They also needed a star. They found their star in Sam Etcheverry, and followed him to heretofore unimagined heights over the 1950s.

When Sam Etcheverry turned out for the freshman football team at high school in Carlsbad, New Mexico, the coach told the boys to line up at the position they usually played. Young Sam had not played any organized football, only pickup on the sandlot, so he lined up at quarterback. There he stayed, through high school and his first three years at Denver University. An inventive but obtuse coach switched him to tailback in a single-wing offence for his senior year in college. That, and his unimposing five-foot, eleven-inch height, may have been the only reasons he was not more highly regarded by the NFL scouts.

Says Etcheverry today, "When I was at Denver University, I didn't even know there was a Canadian football league. The story I got was that Peahead Walker saw a picture of me in a sports magazine and liked the look of my passing motion. They brought me in on the basis of his hunch that I knew how to throw the ball. Lew Hayman had written to my coach advising him they intended to draft me. I didn't know anything about Montreal, but our school had a lot of hockey scholarship players from Quebec and other parts of Canada, and they urged me to go there."

Etcheverry joined the Alouettes for the 1952 season and immediately made an impact. Unfortunately, that impact was a dull thud, the sound of the Alouettes hitting the basement floor as they went 2-10. But Walker and the Als brass had seen enough promise in their young quarterback to have faith that he could turn the team around. He did not disappoint them. The next year, Montreal rebounded to 8-6, good enough for first in the East, but faltered against Hamilton in the two-point eastern final. In

Etcheverry's third year, 1954, they went 11-3, won the East, trounced Hamilton in the playoffs, then entrained for Toronto to take on the western champion Edmonton Eskimos—who were winging eastward in their special-charter forty-eight-passenger Trans-Canada Air Lines North Star—in the Grey Cup game.

Influenced no doubt by the Eskimos' lacklustre showing in the western finals, where they scored only 25 points in the three-game series, and tainted no doubt by central Canadian bias, eastern bookmakers made the Alouettes 5-1 favourites in the contest. They may also have cast an eye over Edmonton's stringbean offensive line, with an average height of six feet and an average weight of only 213 pounds, up against Montreal's big-bird defensive line comprising defensive tackles 265-pound Tex Coulter and 245-pound Jim Staton, among others. On top of everything, Edmonton's first-string quarterback Bernie Faloney was nursing a banged-up knee. But less biased observers would have noted that Edmonton had won eleven regular-season games, the same number as Montreal, and that the team they had barely struggled by in the western final was the defending Grey Cup–champion Winnipeg Blue Bombers.

In every way but one, the Alouettes carried the day. Etcheverry ripped up the Eskimo pass defenders, completing 21 of 31 passes for over 400 yards, more than twice the Edmonton total, including 13 for 316 yards and 2 touchdowns to his favourite beneficiary, the elusive and sure-fingered end John "Red" O'Quinn. All told, the Alouettes outgained the Eskimos by the length of two football fields in total yardage.

Yet they lost. They lost 26-25 to a band of talented opportunists, the most inspired of whom was Jackie Parker, who capitalized on Chuck Hunsinger's disputed fumble. Alone in his dejection in the locker room after the game, Hunsinger pleaded his case. "Sam called our split-42 play. I was supposed to carry the ball around end. Suddenly, I was tackled, but I saw [Alouettes left end] Ray [Poole] and tried to lateral the ball to him. But the ball went forward. It was a forward pass, not a lateral."

Hunsinger's status as MVP on the all-time goat team may or may not be just, but he was not the only Alouette who had stumbled under the Eskimos' relentless pressure. Even O'Quinn had uncharacteristically dropped an end zone pass and coughed up a ball after a completion within scoring range. Peahead Walker put the loss down to "the breaks. We lost the game and nobody could help it. I didn't underestimate them. I knew it would be close, but I thought we could win." Alouettes president Charles Stone reassured Montreal fans: "I know everything's going to be alright. I saw a couple of players smiling and that's a good sign. Wait until next year."

The next year, the Alouettes were hot. Whether it was the fire of determination to avenge their 1954 Grey Cup loss, or simply a matter of the catalytic heat of that particular mix of players with one more season of play together, is moot. What stands without question is that the 1955 Montreal team set about smashing the record books of not just Canadian football but professional football everywhere. Etcheverry's passing yardage and touchdown totals for that season exceeded the NFL records held by the Chicago Bears' legendary Sid Luckman; his completion total eclipsed the 1947 record of NFL Hall of Famer Sammy Baugh. Running back Pasquale "Pat" Abbruzzi's 1,248 yards overshadowed Steve Van Buren's 1949 NFL mark of 1,146. Red O'Quinn's 78 pass receptions rivalled the NFL record of 84 set by the Los Angeles Rams' Tommy Fears in 1953.

The 1955 Montreal team smashed the record books of not just Canadian football but pro football everywhere.

Montreal romped through the regular season with ease, going 9-3. Since they were averaging more than 32 offensive points per game, defence was, to the Alouettes, an afterthought. This one-sided focus in a two-way sport nearly led them to an early exit, though, at the hands of the Toronto Argonauts, upset semi-final winners over Hamilton, in the eastern final. With his team trailing 24-9 at halftime, Peahead Walker had seen enough. "You can either be the biggest team in Canadian football or the biggest bust," he told them. "You've beaten this team four times this season. The trouble is, you're all too tense. You've got the jitters. I want you to relax. This is just another football game. You've got the ammunition," he continued, looking straight at the Rifle. "Go out and play the way you've been doing all season. That's all." And so they did, rolling to a 38-36 victory.

Chastened, the Alouettes were not so cavalier going into the Grey Cup game, held, for the first time, in Vancouver's Empire Stadium. Lest the boys be distracted by the bright lights of the big city, the team lodged up the Fraser River valley at the Dell Motel in the rustic hamlet of Whalley, where they practised against a simulated split-T offence, which they knew Edmonton would employ. Alouettes' scout Joe Zaleski and assistant coach Jimmy Dunn, who had each witnessed a game of the Eskimos' impressive, 55-12, two-game, total-points drubbing of the Blue Bombers in the western final, cautioned that this year's Edmonton team was better than the last.

Montreal practised in secrecy, not wanting to give any edge to their opponents. Peahead Walker was close-mouthed and mysterious in pre-game interviews. One reporter asked, "Your team going to wear cleats, coach?" Walker equivocated, "Yes, and no."

At first, the Alouettes' preparation paid off, as they took a 19-18 lead into the locker room at halftime. Hal Patterson caught 2 touchdown passes, and Pat Abbruzzi crossed the goal-line once, while Bud Korchak added 3 converts and a single, in those days when a touchdown counted for only 5 points. They executed a balanced attack, passing and running equally. Yet they could not shake the persistent Eskimos.

Edmonton coach Pop Ivy assigned rushing defensive left end Frank Anderson, who doubled at offensive guard, to bird-dog Etcheverry all day long. Swatting Anderson away like a pesky gnat, the Montreal pivot connected for an astonishing 508 yards passing. Etcheverry seemed obsessed with his opposite number, Jackie Parker, who had assumed the starting quarterback's role from Bernie Faloney but also played a full game at safety. Constantly, Etcheverry sent receivers into Parker's coverage, resulting in several receptions but also a number of knockdowns and one key interception, just when the Alouettes were moving into scoring territory.

Parker's relentless consistency on both sides of the ball was the hallmark of Edmonton's effort throughout the game. Time and time again, Tex Coulter and linebacker Tom Hugo would converge on the Eskimos' bullish fullback Normie Kwong. Each time, the China Clipper would squirt loose for extra yardage. Parker's legendary ball-handling magic often sent Alouette defenders scrambling after one back while the other carried the ball up the field. The Alouettes' seven-man-line "eagle defence," supposedly adaptable enough to neutralize the Eskimos' split-T offence, laid an egg.

Edmonton's rope-a-dope defence was geared to shutting down the run and denying Montreal the long passes, encouraging Etcheverry to go to the middle short. Having lulled the Alouettes into this pattern in the first half, in the second half the Eskimos stiffened and shut out their frustrated opponents. All the while, the Eskimo offence, with the momentum of a Canadian Pacific locomotive, kept its steam up, doubling its first-half scoring to win 34-19.

Bruised, deflated, dispirited, incredulous, the Alouettes flew back home. Once more, they had played above their best to no avail. The best team in Canada on paper had lost, once again, to the best team on the field. To a man, they vowed it would not happen again.

If the 1955 team had lit a blaze, the 1956 Alouettes unleashed a firestorm on their eastern opponents. They scored 478 points over fourteen league games. Hal Patterson hauled in 88 passes for 1,914 yards, surpassing 100 yards in eleven games. He and Etcheverry connected for a 109-yard touchdown in a September game against Hamilton. Etcheverry, at the peak of his career, completed 276 of 446 attempts for 4,723 yards. Pat Abbruzzi rolled off another 1,000-yard-plus season. This Montreal team scored seemingly at will, racking up 12 touchdowns in one October game against Hamilton. The Alouettes also bulked up their line, acquiring six-foot, five-inch, 275-pound tackle Billy Shipp from Toronto mid-season, to go along with 278-pound tackle Ray Baillie, whom they had acquired from Calgary.

All signs pointed to a Grey Cup rematch against Edmonton, who had won the West with an 11-5 record. Both teams blasted their way into the Cup final, the Eskimos with a 51-7 blowout of the Saskatchewan Rough-riders in the final game of the three-game western final. The Alouettes were reeling from a wild, brawling, 48-41 second game of the eastern final, which saw twenty turnovers, including five Montreal fumbles.

Four thousand Montrealers made the trip to Toronto, certain that this would be the year of atonement. From the opening whistle, it looked as if they would get their wish. Pat Abbruzzi rushed for 117 yards in the first quarter, and the Alouettes scored the game's first touchdown when Hal Patterson ran an end-around to cap a 50-yard drive that had started with Bruce Coulter's interception of a Jackie Parker option pass. Early in the third quarter, the score was tied 20-20.

But then, just as in 1955, Edmonton took their game to another level, and Montreal could not respond. For the first time, Etcheverry appeared human, completing less than half of his passes, perplexed by Edmonton's smothering pass defence and constant pass rush. The Alouette line collapsed under constant pressure from their aggressive, mobile Eskimo counterparts, yielding 459 yards along the ground. Panic set in on the Montreal bench as players saw Edmonton roll to three unanswered touchdowns before Abbruzzi was able to nudge the ball over the line one more time.

Ted Workman's plan was to win a Grey Cup and make Canadian football great.

For the third consecutive year, the Alouettes had fallen to the Eskimos. This time, they had been humiliated, 50-27. On three separate occasions, different Eskimo quarterbacks—Faloney, Parker and Don Getty—had prevailed against the nation's consensus-best quarterback. What made it worse this time around was that the Eskimos had not even felt it necessary to use Parker, their regular-season starting signal-caller, opting instead for Getty, their all-Canadian backup, and shifting Parker to shore up their injury-weakened running back corps. All Getty had done was run for 2 touchdowns and pass for 1 more. Parker had merely rung up a Grey Cup–record 19 points, including 3 touchdowns.

The Alouettes had tried to shore up the middle of their line, but Edmonton tackle Roger Nelson, removing his battle-scarred pads in the Eskimo locker room after the game, bragged that his afternoon's entertainment had been "the easiest line play we had all year. That Shipp, he went down like the *Titanic*." One Montreal player, anonymously, admitted, "Frankly, we're the worst tackling team in the country. It showed up today." Hal Patterson, who had acquitted himself well with two touchdown catches, summed up, in bafflement, the prevalent feeling in the Alouette locker room: "I don't know how, or why, but they beat us good.

We've played better ball games all year. Once could have been lucky, but three times . . ."

The anguish was all too much for Tex Coulter. Two-time all-American from Earl Blaik's West Point powerhouse, six-year veteran of the New York Giants, three-time eastern all-star with the Alouettes, he called it a career two days after Montreal's third straight defeat. Seven-time all-star tackle Herb Trawick, who had been with the team since its formation in 1946, hung up his spikes soon after. The heart had gone out of the eastern champions, and they slipped to 6-8 in 1957. Three years later, O'Quinn and Abbruzzi were gone. Gone, too, was Peahead Walker, the remarkable man who had never played a down at any level but had mastered the game by studying it.

Ted Workman hadn't been just a starry-eyed dilettante when he bought the team in 1956. He brought in serious, sound business ideas about improving both the marketing of the team and the development of the players, particularly Canadian-born players. "My plan was to win a Grey Cup and make football a major sport in French Canada," he would say later. "I wanted to make Canadian football great. I wanted the Montreal Alouettes to be a great Canadian football club. This is where I ran into trouble with Peahead Walker. And this is why I had to fire him."

Walker, the veteran American coach, was the first philosophical wall Workman ran into. Walker was a tyrannical, slow-speaking, mule-stubborn southerner who had no use for Canadian players. He had to have them on his roster, but he didn't have to play them. He preferred to have his imports play two ways. And he was quoted as telling a group of Canadians, on the first day of training camp, "You Canadian boys have a lot of learning to do. I'm not going to teach you, so you better learn fast on your own."

Another time, Walker singled out Chuck Hunsinger, Bill Bewley and Jacques Belec at a practice after a bad loss and told them to form a circle and hold hands. It was a new drill, he said. As the rest of the squad looked on, Walker ordered the three to skip to the left, then to the right, then to jump up and down, still holding hands. After a few minutes of this, he spat on the grass and said, "Look at 'em, dancing and skipping to congratulate themselves on that horse's ass job of blocking they did yesterday."

Workman and his director of player personnel issued a blunt, written operational plan to Walker regarding the use of players. It said that no player should play more than forty minutes a game, that every player dressed should be used, and that Canadian players must be played, "even at the risk of losing a game." Walker coolly ignored the orders and continued to use his Americans both ways. Sportswriter Jim Coleman recalls, "I was looking out from the press box after Tex Coulter launched a punt and who do I see running down with the coverage team but Sam Etcheverry. After the game I asked Peahead why he was using his million-dollar quarterback that way and he just smiled and said, 'That boy just loves to tackle folks.' "

At the end of the 1959 season, after Montreal had been blown out of the playoffs 43-0 by Ottawa, Walker and general manager Gorman Kennedy were fired, and a management consulting company recommended Perry Moss, who had spent one turbulent year as head coach and athletic director at Florida State University. Moss was highly motivated to leave the Sunshine State. Following his Gators' homecoming game loss to William and Mary College in November 1959, students on the Tallahassee campus had hung Moss in effigy, chanting, "Here's to William, here's to Mary. They made a fool out of Perry."

Workman made Moss general manager, and Moss immediately met friction from the veteran imports who had so loved Walker's easy ways. Etcheverry never lost his warm and grateful feelings for the coach who gambled a modest $6,000 initial contract on an obscure quarterback from Denver University and helped boost him to the heights of Canadian football: "He seldom second-guessed me. He never bawled me out. I loved him. He was a great man and a great coach."

Moss, not committed to the forward pass as Walker had been, did not like Etcheverry, thinking him immobile, stubborn and self-centred. Even "Mr. Wonderful" Patterson, regarded as the happiest, quietest superstar in the league, resented Moss's college-style discipline and what he saw as his lack of respect for the veterans.

By 1960, the franchise was seething. And that was the year Workman discovered Moral Re-Armament. He denied that he was ever a card-carrying member of MRA, but he embraced its spiritual tenets in his own life and tried to remould his football team in their image, suggesting to his players that less drinking and less womanizing would make them better players and better people. He bubbled, "Football used to be the end result of my life. But that was superficial. Now I think the Alouettes are designed to illustrate the idealism of MRA." He also said, "Moral Re-Armament is something that gets into you. You don't get into it. It grips you like a passion of the soul."

His players were not buying it. The Montreal media might have dismissed Workman's spiritual rebirth as a harmless quirk, but in another reform-minded move, Workman took the football writers and broadcasters off the pad. For decades, some Montreal sportswriters had received payoffs, monthly envelopes stuffed with folding cash. Workman said later, "Looking back, I should have expected a tougher press after 1960. That was the year I cut off the payment of honorariums to certain sportswriters from the Alouette football club." Tougher was an understatement. The Montreal media were apoplectic. Not only were the bribes stopped, but the tax returns of those on the take were audited and many had to pay back taxes on the extra income. Workman also stopped dispensing free booze at Alouette press conferences, leading to the Canada-wide media cry, "When Workman abstains, everyone abstains."

The once-mighty Alouettes, who had led the East from 1953 through 1956, drifted for a decade, never rising above third place. One of the team's few true stars during the era, running back George Dixon, voted the 1962 CFL player of the year, was out of football by 1965, fallen victim to recurrent injuries.

Deprived of their most luminous marquee star by Etcheverry's departure, the Alouettes sought to sign a big-ticket replacement. For the start of the 1962 season they brought in Sandy Stephens from the University of Minnesota. Personally endorsed by Montreal's chief scout, J. I. Albrecht, Stephens came into town streaming comet-tails of publicity. Upon his graduation from high school in Uniontown, Pennsylvania, fifty-three colleges had recruited him. In 1961 he was selected to five all-America teams and led the Minnesota Gophers to a Rose Bowl victory over UCLA. Ted Workman outbid the New York Titans and the NFL's Cleveland Browns by offering Stephens a three-year, no-cut contract for $115,000.

To say that Stephens was rotund when he came to training camp was to understate it. He had a whiplike arm and bruised people when he ran over them, but he never seemed to be in shape, and he was not a consistent winner. Perry Moss put his faith in Stephens, who did get the Alouettes into the 1962 playoffs, but when they lost to Hamilton, Moss was fired and replaced by the bellicose Jim Trimble. In 1963, Stephens was suspended for failing to trim down to a weight ordered by Trimble. Stephens made a legal challenge to the suspension, which was lifted, but he was subsequently shuttled off to Toronto for the clear-out waiver price of $350. Another quarterback fiasco, another blow to the Alouettes' image.

On December 5, 1967, Workman sold his remaining shares in the team and moved out of the Montreal football offices on the seventeenth floor of Place Ville Marie, taking with him not much but a small bag of mixed emotions. He later wrote, in a two-part, first-person memoir for *Weekend Magazine*, "Most folks can't explain why, but suddenly, thousands—including small children—felt they hated me. They had been assured that I was the source of all their problems . . . I knew [it was time to leave] when I picked up the morning paper, November 7, 1967. The headline screamed MAN AGAINST A CITY. What goes on in a man's heart when he reads that kind of a story about himself? Because I had now endured eight seasons of this sort of guerilla warfare I suppose I should have retreated into a shell. But I didn't. I felt myself getting hotter as I read on. It hurt like hell. . .

"It may be that, on moral issues, I did have some issues with one or more of the Alouette players or coaches. Many of the stories that have gone the rounds are either gross distortions or outright lies. All I tried to do was make the team aware of its responsibility to deport itself in a way that would reflect credit on the members and set an example that others —especially youth—could profitably follow. Isn't it the job of football to build character?"

On the botched trade, he wrote, "It was a tough decision. We knew there would be a public outcry. But if you owned the Alouettes at the time, and given the same set of circumstances, what would you have done? I knew what I had to do."

In 1970, new owner Sam Berger sought to recapture some of the magic of the mid-1950s by elevating Sam Etcheverry to head coach. Etcheverry had coached the short-lived Montreal Rifles of the Continental Football League and then joined the Alouettes as an assistant coach. Berger guaranteed him a free hand, and Etcheverry used it to sweep the locker room clean, bringing in twenty-three new players, as well as his old passing mate Red O'Quinn from Ottawa as general manager.

The Alouettes finished the 1970 season in third place, but they surprised Toronto, 16-7, in the eastern semi-final, then surprised themselves by besting the regular-season-leading Ti-Cats in the two-game eastern finals. Much to their amazement, and that of onlookers, the Alouettes found themselves in Toronto for the Grey Cup facing the Calgary Stampeders, who, like them, had somehow finessed a third-place finish into a final berth.

Just before the start of the eastern playoffs, Etcheverry, a hard-line disciplinarian, took a ferocious gamble, suspending two of his starters, import fullback Dennis Duncan and Canadian receiver Bob McCarthy, for repeated curfew violations. The step might have shattered the team, but instead it welded the players solidly to Etcheverry.

Berger guaranteed Etcheverry a free hand, and he used it to sweep the locker room clean.

The Alouettes' unlikely field general for the Grey Cup game was Jesse Wade, Jr., better known as Sonny. Montreal had plucked the myopic Wade from microscopic Emory & Henry College in Virginia, where in his senior year the six-foot, three-and-a-half-inch Wade had drawn the attention of pro scouts by driving the Wasps to an average of 542 yards per game. The late-season acquisition of contact lenses had improved Wade's performance immeasurably. "They helped my depth perception," he said later. "Before I used the lenses, some of my pass receivers looked blurry around the edges."

In the early stages of the 1970 Grey Cup game, Montreal fans might have suspected Wade's oculist was a Calgary booster, as the Alouettes looked anything but champions. Wade's first pass was intercepted, and the Stampeders scored the afternoon's first touchdown five minutes into the first period after Montreal halfback Bob Storey fumbled away a punt return. Then, inadvertently, one Alouette ended up in the Calgary end zone with the ball in his hands.

Late in the first quarter, backup receiver Ted Alflen carried in a message from the bench, suggesting Wade try a long count to pull the overeager Calgary pass rushers offside. Alflen had to stay in for one play, so he ran a decoy pattern out wide. The ball went to running back Moses Denson, who was snared by Calgary defensive back Terry Wilson behind the line of scrimmage. As Wilson was pulling him down by the ankle, Denson looked around for an outlet.

Alflen had wandered into the end zone on a made-up route. "I looked back and saw Moses was stopped," Alflen recalled. "Then I saw him raise his arm and I thought, 'He's going to throw me the ball,' so I started to run." Alflen crossed the goal-line, and George Springate's convert tied the game.

The Alouettes scored the only other touchdown they would need in the third quarter on a bottom-of-the-bag trick play called a 36-Slant R Reverse Left, a play Montreal had not used since early in the season. Alouette receivers Ted Alflen, Peter Dalla Riva and Bruce Van Ness ran clearing patterns on the left side, drawing Calgary defenders Jim Furlong, Greg Perez and Larry Robinson with them. Wade rolled out right, stumbled on a muffin of torn-up turf, then bootlegged the ball to right-side slotback Tom Pullen, who reversed his field and darted around left behind the blocking of the pulling guard and the tackle, Pierre Desjardins and Ed George, 7 yards for the score. Wade threw a clinching touchdown to Gary Lefebvre in the final quarter, and the Alouettes coasted to a 23-10 win.

Sonny Wade left CNE Stadium field that afternoon with the game's MVP award, the keys to a new car and a renewed faith in the science of optometry. When he and his teammates landed in Montreal, 5,000 delirious fans met them, venting two decades of frustration with a cele-bratory yelp. First off the plane was Miss Grey Cup, the reigning Miss Alouette, Nancy Durrell. Following close behind her, leading his team down the ramp as they acknowledged the cheers and chants of the crowd, was the Alouettes' victorious head coach, Sam Etcheverry, his Grey Cup dream fulfilled at last.

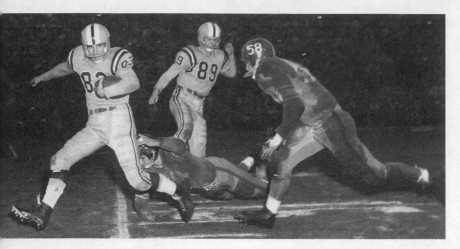

Previous page: Hamilton and Winnipeg sparred for dominance throughout the late 1950s and early 1960s. Field general of the Blue Bombers over his 11-year career was Ken Ploen (#89), who led Winnipeg to three of its four Grey Cups between 1958 and 1962. VANCOUVER SUN

Both teams boasted a nucleus of aggressive, durable veterans. *Above:* The Bombers built upon a strong foundation of Manitoba players. From 1957 through 1967, Winnipeg native Cornell Piper (#58) held steady at guard. VANCOUVER SUN

Right: A rare offensive highlight for a defensive all-star, as Ti-Cats all-star lineman John Barrow scores a touchdown against Ottawa. Over his 14-year career, Barrow went to the Grey Cup nine times. CFHF

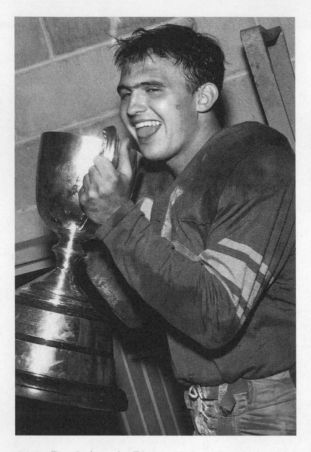

Right: Bracketing the Blue Bomber offensive line were two exceptionally talented ends: Farrell Funston *(left)* and Ernie Pitts *(centre)*. Both played hard, on and off the field. Funston, a free spirit, kept the team loose in the dressing room, and in after-hours activities. Pitts, with a reputation as a ladies' man, cut a wide swath through both the backfields and the bars of western Canada. CFHF

Above: Baby-faced hero of the 1958 Grey Cup, Winnipeg quarterback Jim Van Pelt, a rival for Ploen in the late 1950s, had his promising career cut short by service in the U.S. military.
VANCOUVER SUN

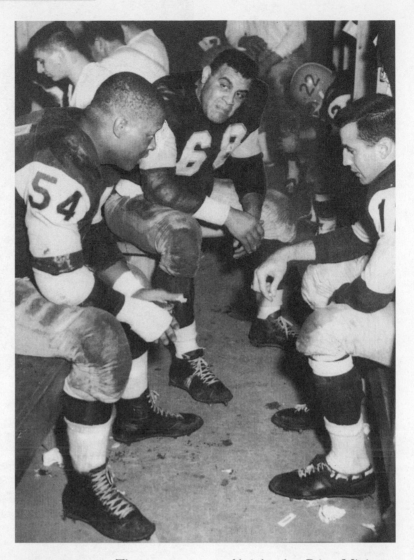

The prospect appeared bright when Prime Minister John Diefenbaker *(inset)* approached the ball for the ceremonial kickoff at the 1962 Grey Cup game. But soon, mists drifting in off Lake Ontario obscured vision so badly for players like Blue Bombers running back Leo Lewis *(left)* that CFL Commissioner Sidney Halter reluctantly stopped play. The balance of the game was played the next day, with Winnipeg prevailing 28–27. CFHF

Above: After the game on Sunday, the second time they had suited up in twenty-four hours, Ti-Cats Ellison Kelly (#54), Angelo Mosca (#68) and Frank Cosentino (#11) slumped, dejected, in their dressing room. CANAPRESS PHOTO SERVICE

Flushed with enthusiasm and boasting a brand-new stadium built for the British Empire Games, the B.C. Lions joined the fray in 1954. Head coach and general manager Annis Stukus, a tireless promoter, drummed up popular support for the new franchise through an endless round of public appearances and "media events." Here he poses for the cameras with some of the first Lions *(l–r)* Johnny Mazur, Pete Thodos and Arnie Weinmeister. A star in the United States before returning to his home country, Weinmeister is a member of the NFL Hall of Fame. B.C. SPORTS HALL OF FAME

Below: Another original Lion, Norm Fieldgate, was still on the team when B.C. won its first Grey Cup in 1964. VANCOUVER SUN

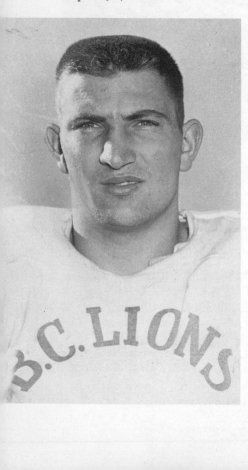

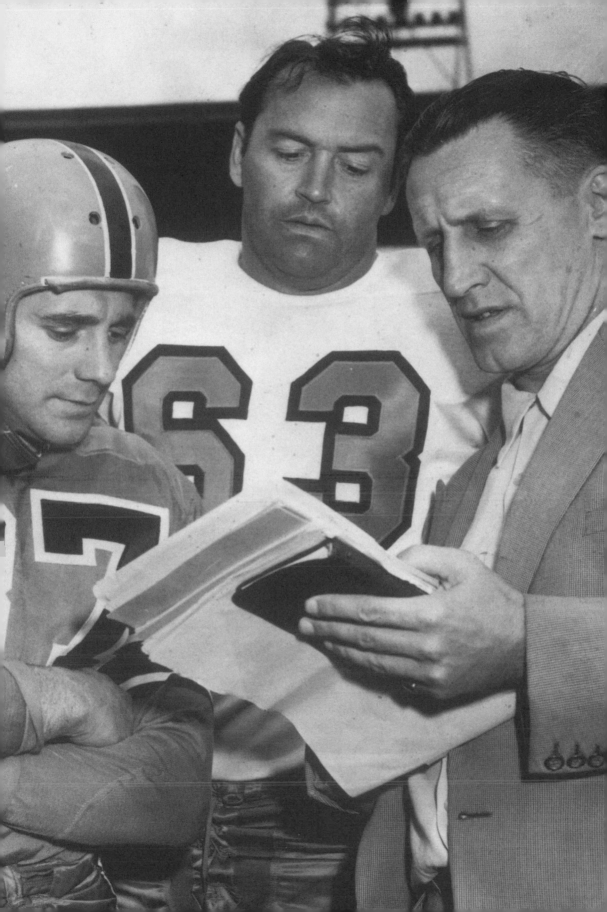

Right: Fearless in the pocket despite his oft-injured knees, quarterback Joe Kapp (#22) led the Lions to their first Grey Cup in their tenth season. Three decades later, Kapp returned to the Lions as head coach.
BRIAN KENT/VANCOUVER SUN

Above: A stalwart on those early Lions teams, and for many years after, was By Bailey (38). A consummate team player, Bailey switched from the offensive to defensive backfield, making an outstanding contribution wherever he played. BILL CUNNINGHAM/ THE PROVINCE

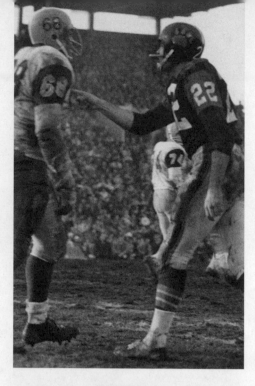

Top right: Caught in the act on a play that to this day raises the ire of Lions faithful, Hamilton's terminator Angelo Mosca lunges into downed B.C. running back Willie Fleming (#15) early in the 1963 Grey Cup. CFHF

Bottom right: Helped to the sidelines by trainer Roy Cavallin *(right)*, Fleming never returned to the game. The

Empire Stadium crowd was livid, calling for Mosca's head. BRIAN KENT/ VANCOUVER SUN

Top left: Hot under the collar, Joe Kapp accuses Mosca of a late hit. THE PROVINCE

Bottom left: Mosca later capitalized on his notoriety to promote a pro wrestling career. NORTHWEST WRESTLING PROMOTIONS

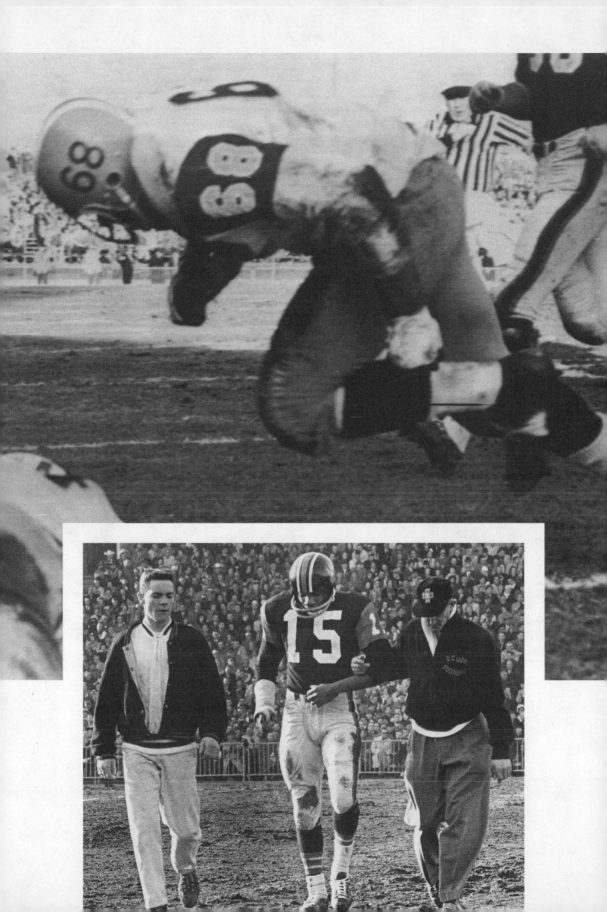

Fans of Canadian football have always thrilled to the ingenuity and sheer athleticism of the game's running backs, but no one type of runner has predominated.

Above: Saskatchewan's George Reed, who led the league in rushing five straight years from 1965–69, would plunge straight ahead, daring tacklers to get in his way. *Left:* The Bombers' balletic Leo Lewis (#29) would cut back and dart for daylight. CFHF

Overleaf: Ron Stewart's agile, compact frame let him elude less mobile opposing linemen. Stewart's single-game rushing record of 287 yards still stands today. CFHF

CHAPTER FIVE

Working-Class Warriors: Hamilton Tiger-Cats

Queen Elizabeth Way, Canada's first four-lane superhighway, built in the 1930s at a then-staggering cost of $1 million a mile, links two of the oldest Canadian Football League franchises like a set of leg irons. At one end, Toronto, illuminated by big-city bright lights and its own lurid sense of itself. At the other, Hamilton, brooding in the shadow of the big town forty miles up the road, lit by resentment and the roaring flames of its steel mills.

In all its pursuits—politics, the arts, media and sports—Toronto, as Canada's largest city, has always manifested a visible sense of entitlement that sets role-model targets for some Canadian cities and causes seething resentment in many others. Toronto drives Hamiltonians bonkers, and nowhere is this expressed more viscerally than on the football field. Since the founding of the Hamilton Tigers in 1869, Hamilton teams have won fourteen Grey Cups. Since the 1873 founding of the Toronto Argonauts Football Club by the Toronto Argonaut Rowing Club, Toronto teams have won twenty. During and in between those singular successes, the two lakeside teams have been at each other's throats.

Hamilton's fanatical fan support, and innate antipathy to the Argonauts, goes back to the second Grey Cup game, in 1910, the Tigers against Varsity. The sponsoring Hamilton Amateur Athletic Association offered club memberships the week of the national final, five hundred of them available at $5, permitting members first call on tickets a day before the general sale. All five hundred memberships were sold in a few hours. The Toronto *Globe* reported on the frenzied demand for general game tickets: "As early as six p.m. Monday, boys and old men began to gather in front of Stanley Mills's store and before midnight the line extended down Hughson Street. Camp stools, biscuit boxes and orange crates were used as seats and the big gathering passed the cold dreary night as best they could, cracking jokes and comforted by the hope that when morning came they would be well-rewarded. Some late arrivals paid as much as $2 for a place in line to secure a 50-cent bleacher seat. Grandstand seats brought $5 during the morning and some who were anxious to witness the game paid as much as $15 a pair."

A crowd of 12,000 jammed the Hamilton cricket grounds; hundreds who didn't have tickets knocked down the fences and perched on the scoreboard to watch in disappointment as Varsity beat Hamilton, coached by Seppi DuMoulin and Chaucer Elliot, 16-7. Two Hamilton papers that planned to have Extras available at game's end were unable to print—all their printers and engravers had abandoned the presses to attend the game.

Vancouver journalist Trevor Lautens, who grew up on the Mountain in Hamilton before coming west in 1963, says today, "The city of Hamilton was nuts about its football team. The relationship between the city and the Tiger-Cats was extremely close. The football culture was essential to the identity of a city that seemed to be in the shadow of Toronto in every way. Hamilton has always been the most overlooked city in the world. Beyond the steel industry, football was the city's one source of pride. Nothing better could happen to a Hamilton kid than to run into a Tiger-Cat player at Max Mintz's Chicken Roost and be able to talk to him about the next game. And the Labour Day home-and-home double-header with Toronto was always the social event of the year in Hamilton."

John Barrow, who put in fourteen brilliant seasons for Hamilton—he was versatile enough to play six positions and was a 1962 Schenley Award winner—put it more succinctly: "I have always tried to play with Hamilton spirit." This sense of place, or civic pride, resulted not only in extraordinary team success but in careers that extended far beyond the playing years. Ti-Cat players came to play; they remained to become suc-cessful citizens.

Fans associated the Tabbies with something along the lines of legalized mayhem.

Hamilton teams of the 1950s and early 1960s were a dynamic blend of offensive power and defensive might, led on the field by hard-nosed backfielders and storming defensive players. Their style was as tough and abrasive as the steel-making city they called home. Hamilton was a brawling, energetic town, populated by people of Polish, Italian, Baltic, Dutch, German and Portuguese extraction who packed their lunch buckets to Stelco, Defasco, International Harvester, National Steel Car and Otis Elevator work sites and put in an honest eight hours. On weekends, they expected their football team to be as honest.

By the 1950s, Hamilton's steel mills had converted from the wartime production that had spawned their expansion to forge the raw steel that fuelled a postwar construction boom then sweeping Canada. People worked hard. The heat from the blast furnaces, the smoke from the retorts, toughened the skin and blackened the lungs. On days off, many workers sought release through football. They bellowed support for their team, whose black and yellow uniforms were a reminder of the roaring fires that glowed at night from the factories along the lakeshore, the dark clouds that spewed skyward from tall chimneys. Hamilton football fans were not interested in the cerebral strategies of inner football; they wanted to see a Hamilton player hit an opposing player hard enough to knock his helmet and his courage flying.

Former Canadian Press sports editor Jack Sullivan wrote, in his 1970 book *The Grey Cup Story*, "Over the years Hamilton picked up the reputation of producing tough, rough football teams befitting a steel town. The system wasn't sophisticated, nothing like the Old School Tie aura that surrounds the Toronto Argonauts or the Rough Riders of Ottawa. Fans associated the Tabbies with something along the lines of legalized mayhem."

If the personality of an individual, group or nation can be established in an instant, then it might be said that the essential granite-knuckle disposition of the Hamilton Tiger-Cats was genetically imprinted in the dying seconds of the 1953 Grey Cup game, when Hamilton tackler Lou Kusserow's helmet and shoulders smashed into Winnipeg receiver Tom Casey's ribcage on the Hamilton 1-yard line. The impact was permanent.

It was appropriate that a defensive player made the decisive play that clinched Hamilton's first Grey Cup triumph. A rock-hard defence, as solid and impenetrable as the Niagara Escarpment that skirts the rugged steeltown, was at the core of the football philosophy of Carl Voyles, the Florida tomato farmer who planted the seed that would yield ten Grey Cup appearances, including four victories, over the next fifteen years.

Carl M. "Dutch" Voyles was a soft-spoken man with bushy eyebrows that perched above a penetrating gaze. When he talked at all, it was in simple, plain-spoken home truths. "Little details make for good football." "You must adapt your plays to your players." And he spoke of desire: "A man either has it or he hasn't. You can't teach him that." Platitudes, perhaps. But they had been tried and proven through thirty years of football coaching at every level, most recently with the Brooklyn Dodgers of the All-America Football Conference. After the collapse of that franchise in 1949, Voyles had returned to his Vero Beach, Florida, tomato farm in search of a less stressful life.

When the directors of the newly merged Tiger-Cat franchise sought NFL commissioner Bert Bell's opinion on who he considered the best football coach available, Bell named Voyles. At first, Voyles demurred, but after being offered the combined position of head coach and general manager and promised a free hand to reorganize the team as he saw fit, he accepted the challenge, beginning with the 1950 season.

Amalgamation had come about as the two existing franchises, the Hamilton Tigers of the Ontario Rugby Football Union (ORFU) and the Hamilton Wildcats of the Big Four, faced up to the fiscal impossibility of operating two profitable franchises in a city of barely 170,000 people. Both teams had distinguished histories. The Tigers had played in that second-ever Grey Cup, losing on that muddy winter day in 1910 to Varsity. They won the Cup in 1913 and went on to pick up four more national titles in the prewar years. The Wildcats had won two of the wartime Cups. But since the war both had fallen on hard times, the Tigers having finished dead last in every season since hostilities ended, winning a grand total of three of forty-eight games over four seasons.

Voyles turned Hamilton's fortunes around in one season. The 1950 Tiger-Cats, with Voyles at the helm, had an all-star lineup including end Vince Mazza, guard Vince Scott and tackle Ralph Sazio, whom Voyles had coached in Brooklyn. The team, captained by ten-year veteran centre Jake Gaudaur, finished first in the East before losing to Toronto in the Big Four final.

In 1997, Gaudaur recalled one early incident that, ultimately, forged a remarkable chain of command. "As I was the team captain, Voyles asked me to take this tackle, Ralph Sazio, to lunch and convince him to sign and stay on in Hamilton. I guess I did a pretty good selling job because Ralph stayed on to play, to coach and then to succeed me as president and general manager. But, you know, I never got reimbursed for that lunch."

With the arrival of Voyles, a pattern was set. A core of reliable players signed on, and the Tiger-Cats would finish no worse than second in the East for the balance of the 1950s. In 1953, Voyles took the team to his first Grey Cup game, against the Winnipeg Blue Bombers. The Tiger-Cats had finished tied for first with Montreal, but had outscored the Alouettes 59-23 in the two-game, total points eastern final. Montreal's frustration had overflowed on the sideline late in the second game, when Red O'Quinn jumped to his feet from the bench and tackled Hamilton's Bernie Custis, who was on his way to a certain touchdown. It was a token gesture, as the Ti-Cats were awarded the ball on the Montreal 3 and scored regardless.

An air of smugness surrounded the Hamilton fans as they settled into

Varsity Stadium, home of their hated and pointedly absent rivals, for the Grey Cup game. Hamilton scored first on that clear November day, ten minutes into the game, on a quarterback sneak by Ed Songin. The lead held up until the third quarter, when Bomber fullback Gerry James plunged in from the 1-yard line. Moments later, fading back to midfield, Songin lofted a pass to Vito Ragazzo over the head of rookie defender Geoff Crane, and Ragazzo ran untouched into the end zone.

Still, in the closing moments of the game, it looked as if Winnipeg had a chance to tie. Bomber quarterback Jack Jacobs put together an inspired drive, leading his team from their own 5-yard line to the Ti-Cats' 5. Then, with seconds left, he tried one last pass to Casey at the goal-line. Kusserow, who had been assigned to cover Bomber receiver Neill Armstrong, took a calculated, split-second gamble, leaving Armstrong in the end zone and smashing into Casey just as the ball arrived. The ball hit the turf, the gun sounded and Hamilton had its first Grey Cup.

The Bombers were outraged, claiming Kusserow had hit Casey before the ball arrived. Game films showed the hit was legal, but deep enmity began to fester between the two teams. It would have to wait, as neither team made the final for another three years while Edmonton and Montreal began their celebrated rivalry.

That Grey Cup victory came as a long-service reward to Jake Gaudaur. He had retired after the 1951 season and had been a team director for two years. But when Hamilton's import centre went down with injuries in the 1953 season, Gaudaur strapped on the armour for one more rewarding season. By the time Hamilton and Winnipeg met again, Voyles had gone back home to his tomato fields, Gaudaur was Hamilton's general manager, and the new coach was a meaty slab of controversy, Jim Trimble.

As general manager, Gaudaur made two key moves, among many, that were to set in motion a Ti-Cat juggernaut that would dominate the East for more than a decade. In 1956 he hired Trimble, who fit the Hamilton mould perfectly: a native of McKeesport, Pennsylvania, he had worked in the steel mills there as a youth and had a hard-labour attitude to football. The second move followed the discovery by Gaudaur and Trimble that the Edmonton Eskimos had left quarterback Bernie Faloney off their protected list while he served a mandatory two years in the U.S. armed services. Hamilton pounced, claiming him on waivers. Edmonton, with Jackie Parker switched permanently to quarterback and Canadian Don Getty available as his backup, didn't need Faloney, but to let him get away with nothing in return turned out to be a monstrous mistake.

Trimble arrived in Hamilton with a larger-than-life, swaggering reputation and a tongue that never rested. As head coach of the Philadelphia Eagles, he had been voted NFL coach of the year in 1952. By 1955, his lack of diplomacy had so alienated his players and the Philadelphia ownership—he said of one popular running back, "That guy is so dumb he couldn't pour piss out of a boot if the instructions were printed on the heel"—that he was fired. Actually, the management decision was prompted by a player revolt led by Lum Snyder, who was called "the best tackle in the National Football League" by the great Cleveland Browns coach Paul Brown. When the demanding Trimble twice fined Snyder for late-hit penalties, Snyder announced he was retiring because he couldn't live with Trimble. Veteran quarterback Bobby Thomason and all-star centre Chuck Bednarik stood with Snyder in the revolt, and Trimble was gone. Based on another tip from Bert Bell, Gaudaur invited Trimble north. Snyder later became an assistant coach with the B.C. Lions in 1959.

A rock as a player, Trimble was the same as a coach, occasionally throwing his six-foot-two, 250-pound body into scrimmages to show how he wanted it done. He was not given to chatty discourse with his players. Gaudaur recalls, "I sold Cookie Gilchrist to Saskatchewan the day after he challenged Trimble to a fistfight after a practice. I don't think Cookie realized how kind I was being to him."

It was about this time that Jim Coleman, the witty, syndicated sports columnist, characterized the Ti-Cats as "large, healthy chaps who delight in clasping an opponent against their manly bosoms and squeezing until the opponent's blood squirts from his ears." Under Trimble, with Gaudaur's timely signings of combative players like Ralph Goldston, Angelo Mosca and John Barrow, the team became even more ill-mannered. And with Trimble's direction the results began to show. In the 1957 season, the Hamilton defence held its opponents to an average of fewer than 14 points a game in the regular season. The Ti-Cat offence contributed fewer than 18 points per game, but the combined result was good enough to win the East. When it counted, in the playoffs, the offence under Bernie Faloney clicked, demolishing the Montreal Alouettes 39-1 in the second game of the eastern final.

After three seasons in which the Grey Cup game became an exclusive grudge match between Montreal and Edmonton, two new dancing partners emerged. Winnipeg had sandbagged Edmonton in the western final and headed east to meet the Ti-Cats, again at Varsity Stadium. The game was a homecoming of sorts for Trimble and Winnipeg coaches Bud Grant and Wayne Robinson, who had played for Trimble in Philadelphia. It would be the first of five times that Grant, the pupil, and Trimble, the teacher, would contest the national title.

Hamilton quickly knocked the Bombers off balance as Ray "Bibbles" Bawel scooped up a Winnipeg fumble at midfield and ran it in for a score. Bawel, who had also played for Trimble in Philly, bagged another fumble and intercepted two passes during the game.

Scoreless and trailing by 2 converted touchdowns at the half, Winnipeg started the third quarter with a drive to Hamilton's 5. But running back Gerry James, playing with a fractured hand suffered in the first quarter, lost the ball—one of three fumbles he made that day. The play was eerily similar to one involving James's father, the great "Dynamite Eddie" James, a quarter of a century earlier in the 1931 Grey Cup game against the Winged Wheelers. In that game, the Winged Wheelers led by 2 touchdowns at the half. To open the second half, the senior James, for the Bombers, spearheaded a drive deep into Montreal territory. He broke clear, with no one in front of him, but unaccountably lost the handle on the ball at the Montreal 24. The Wheelers recovered and drove back up field, cruising to a 22-0 victory.

Just as in 1931, the 1957 Blue Bombers never recovered from this reversal of fortune, but James was not solely responsible. He and his teammates, roughhoused by the brawling Hamilton defence, turned the ball over eight times. Hamilton got the offence it needed from a pair of powerhouses, Cookie Gilchrist and Gerry McDougall, running backs the size of linebackers.

McDougall, a rookie from UCLA, rushed for over 1,000 yards in his first season, 1957, and scored 2 touchdowns in the windup of the eastern final. As for Gilchrist, who had not played college ball before signing with the Cleveland Browns in 1953, he might have been the greatest two-way player ever in Canada, except he had what would be labelled in the 1990s as "attitude." He played for three teams in the U.S. and five in Canada. In his time with the Buffalo Bills, Gilchrist demanded a chauffeur-driven limousine with a telephone. As a compromise, he got a leased car, driven by a taxi-squad rookie, and the telephone. The driver was instructed that when the phone rang, he was to say, "Mr. Gilchrist's car. Mr. Gilchrist? Hold on, please, I'll see if he's in."

One of the most bizarre plays in Grey Cup history came in the last quarter when Bawel jumped in front of Ernie Pitts and intercepted a pass. Running down the sideline with nothing but Ontario air in front of him, he was tripped up by a spectator as he passed the Bomber bench. Referee Paul Dojack penalized the Bombers half the distance to the goal-line. But by then it was academic; Hamilton cruised to a 32-7 victory. After the game, Bawel showed reporters a smudge of brown civilian shoe polish on one of his white socks. Later, the culprit was identified as a prominent Toronto lawyer. Still later, Bawel received in the mail a gold watch and a note saying, "From the Tripper. Grey Cup 1957."

But Grant got his revenge on Trimble. Four times over the next five years the same teams met in the Grey Cup, and Grant's Bombers won all four of them. The 1958 final was a squeaker, 35-28; 1959 was a 21-7 walkover. In 1960 the dispirited Ti-Cats slumped to last place in the East. But Hamilton was back in first place the following year with a 10-4 record.

One reason for the resurgence was the pass-catching of Hal Patterson, appearing courtesy of Ted Workman's generosity. Patterson had been a deep threat for Montreal for seven seasons, and he didn't break stride upon his move to Hamilton, combining with Faloney on game-breaker passes. Patterson was a Canadian all-star at wide receiver from 1962 through 1964. (Jake Gaudaur seemed to have a demonic ability to flim-flam Workman. In addition to stealing Patterson, Gaudaur, in an interview for this book, referred to a later agreement as the time "when I was able to talk Ted Workman into taking Trimble off my hands.")

The Tiger-Cats had won ninety-nine regular season games and lost fifty-nine since the plain-speaking Carl Voyles had outlined strategies on a chalkboard in 1950. The only thing they hadn't done was adapt to changing times. They were complacent. And things were changing. The age of the specialist was upon the CFL. Hamilton was still using many players both ways. Bomber coach Bud Grant, by contrast, referred proudly to "my thirty-four first-stringers."

Hamilton scored early in the 1961 Grey Cup game and held a 14-7 lead after three quarters. But fatigue ambushed them. They began to clank and wheeze. The younger, fresher Bombers scored to tie it and force the first overtime in almost half a century of Grey Cup play. Thirteen of Winnipeg's 14 points in regulation time—a touchdown, 2 field goals and a convert—were scored by Gerry James. Nearing the end of his career, James more than made up for his disgrace in the 1957 game.

Overtime was two ten-minute periods, and that was too much for Hamilton, who had gone into extra time against the Argos a week earlier. Early in the second extra period, Bomber quarterback Kenny Ploen ran in an 18-yard touchdown that ended it. "Hell of a bruising game," said Trimble. "Real tough."

The Hamilton players took a post-game vow that it wouldn't happen again. But it did. The following year. And this one took even longer to lose: two days. An uncharacteristic spell of warm weather had generated a swirling mist on Lake Ontario. A few hundred yards from the lakeside stadium, the air was sparkling clear. But a breeze blowing inland carried fog banks that blanketed the field. Players at field level could see well enough to function, but in the seats, 32,655 spectators didn't have a view or a clue.

Sitting on a rolled-up tarpaulin at field level, G. Sydney Halter was squirming on a horned dilemma. The CFL commissioner had an obligation to the American Broadcasting Corporation, which had paid $36,000 to carry the 1962 Grey Cup game to the estimated 22 million viewers of *Wide World of Sports* in the United States. On the other hand, there were those 32,000 fans in the stands. The minority carried, and with nine minutes and twenty-two seconds left in the fourth quarter, and Winnipeg leading 28-27, Halter called a long time out. They would finish the game the following day. The decision was unprecedented in Canadian senior professional football.

And so on Sunday they picked up where they had left off on Saturday.

Only 15,000 fans showed up back for the rump session. But those who flew home or stayed home didn't miss much. There was no further scoring Sunday, and Winnipeg had its 1-point victory, twenty-four and three-quarter hours after the opening kickoff.

In six seasons, Trimble had finished first in the East five times; he had gone to five Grey Cups but had won just one, in 1957. That wasn't good enough. As he moved to Montreal after the 1962 season, he said with remarkable good grace, "Maybe now the Tiger-Cats can get a coach who can beat Bud Grant."

Howling winds gusted up to fifty miles an hour, making every punt an adventure.

As he did in all things, Jake Gaudaur weighed the options and made a status quo decision. He opted not to gut the team and to maintain continuity at the coaching level. He chose Ralph Sazio, who had come to Hamilton in 1950 and never left, becoming an assistant coach in 1953.

Sazio didn't rebuild. He fine-tuned and improved, making only five roster changes from the previous year. He added Art Baker, a tough running back from the Buffalo Bills camp. Halfback Tommy Grant, of Windsor, Ontario, became the deep-threat receiver of choice. The maturing Garney Henley led the league in pass interceptions. John Barrow and Angelo Mosca anchored the defence in all-Canada style. That year Hamilton was back in the Grey Cup, this time in Vancouver against a battered B.C. Lions team. Hamilton won 21-10 in a one-sided game in which Mosca, on a marginally late hit on Lions halfback Willie Fleming, earned the hatred of all living west of the B.C-Alberta border. It was turnabout in 1964, the Lions beating Hamilton 34-24 on a blustery day in Toronto, with one of the key—and redeeming—plays being Fleming's 68-yard scoring burst over tackle as Mosca was wiped out by a trap block by B.C.'s all-star tackle Lonnie Dennis.

Things changed for the Tiger-Cats in 1965. The weather got worse, but their Grey Cup fortunes improved. There was no fog this time. What rolled in from Lake Ontario instead were howling winds that gusted up to fifty miles an hour, making every punt an adventure. One of Bomber Ed Ulmer's punts rocketed up off his foot, slowed, stopped and came back to him. Bomber coach Bud Grant, unwilling to risk blow-back punts on third down in his own end of the field, three times conceded safeties by having his punter run back into his own end zone. He gave up 2 points each time, but he retained possession. However, while the logic may have been sound, the outcome led many to second-guess him. Hamilton won the game 22-16, the 6-point margin being precisely the number of charity points Grant had conceded. It took an act of God, but the Ti-Cats had finally beaten the Bombers in a Grey Cup game.

Tiger-Cat players of the 1950s and 1960s went one step further than Julius Caesar: they came, they saw, they conquered—and they stayed on. The loyalty and long-term commitment Hamilton had extended to its players were reciprocated by the players themselves. In a 1997 *Maclean's* column, Hamilton coach Don Sutherin, the former defensive back and kicker, was recounting for writer Trent Frayne the astonishing story of the 1961 Hamilton team's comeback victory in the eastern final against Toronto. He concluded by telling Frayne, "A lot of those guys are still here. Faloney's here. Angelo Mosca's here, Ellison Kelly's here. John Barrow went back to Texas for a while, but he's moving back. Lot of other guys who came up here are still here—Tommy Joe Coffey, Bernie Ruoff, Dave Marler, Willie Bethea."

The same year, at testimonial dinners held in the Hamilton area for Bernie Custis and Ellison Kelly, Jake Gaudaur recalled, "Bernie Custis was the first black quarterback to play in Canada. He played three or four years with us, taught school here and retired as a principal. And Ellison Kelly, it seems like it was just last year that I rushed out to the New York Giants training camp in Disneyland to sign him, but it was actually thirty-seven years ago."

Gaudaur has been around the steel city a long time himself. Born in Orillia, he had no interest in football when he first came to Hamilton as a nineteen-year-old, 210-pound lacrosse star and Canadian champion oarsman. Accepting a challenge, he attended the Hamilton training camp in 1940, made the club and stayed in the game for forty-four years: fourteen as a player, fourteen as a team executive and sixteen as the league commissioner. He was inducted into the Canadian Football Hall of Fame in 1984. His Hamilton teams won nine eastern titles and four Grey Cups.

When Gaudaur took over as commissioner in 1967, the CFL drew 1.5 million fans. The year he retired, in 1984, attendance was 3 million. In 1967, CFL revenues were $8 million. When Gaudaur left, they were $44 million. The 1967 Grey Cup earned $300,000 in revenue; the 1983 Grey Cup game $2.5 million. In 1967, CFL television revenues were $750,000; in 1984 they were $11 million.

Today, Gaudaur speaks fondly of his adopted city. "No doubt about it, we tend to stay here longer than players in other cities. The personality of the community was always a major factor in that. We were always able to find good jobs for the players and a lot of them built very successful careers. We might be described as the Pittsburgh of Canada, thousands of workers turning out steel products. In the fourteen years that I ran the team, I always favoured big, tough, defensive players and the city seemed to like that. And we took care of our players. I remember, when I was trying to find a job for Angelo Mosca, I sent him out to McMaster University to take an IQ test. He got one of the highest scores the testing board had ever registered."

Bernie Faloney, who played for Edmonton, Hamilton, Montreal and the B.C. Lions, always came back to the Hamilton area. Today he lives in Burlington as the semi-retired president and CEO of Contractors Machinery and Equipment Ltd. and affiliated CME Industries, heavy equipment and lift companies that he joined as a salesman while still playing football. He kept buying small pieces of the companies until he owned them, and he has now handed over the daily operation to his sons, Wally and Bernie, Jr. "I just deal with the bankers," he says. "Bankers seem to prefer dealing with a guy with some grey in his hair.

"I've had a great life in Hamilton, in football and in business. When I first got here, there wasn't a hell of a lot else for people to do so they gathered around the football team. It was very close knit."

Faloney's playing career was extraordinary, the more so because so much of it was inadvertent. He never planned to spend his young life playing football. But sheer twists of fate involved him in what were probably the two most unusual plays in the history of modern Canadian football: the Run (Western Division) and the Run (Eastern Division).

An all-America split-T quarterback at the University of Maryland,

Faloney was the first draft choice of the San Francisco 49ers in his senior year. "They still had Y. A. Tittle in his prime," he recalls, "so I knew I wouldn't be playing much if I went there. Plus they only offered me $9,000, which wasn't much for a first draft. And I really didn't know how long I wanted to play. Jan and I were just married and I thought it would be nice to earn enough for a down payment on a house, and then get on with something else.

"But Pop Ivy phoned from Edmonton after we played in the Orange Bowl and said I should come to Canada and play the split-T for him. After that [club president] Al Anderson came down, wearing his big white cowboy hat, and just said, 'What do you want?' I said, 'Give me $12,000 in Canadian dollars'—which were at a 10 per cent premium in those days—'$1,000 to sign and a per-game salary in the playoffs.' We settled it all in one day."

It's a little-known fact that Faloney was the third quarterback on the field during the Run (Western Division), Jackie Parker's dramatic touchdown return of Chuck Hunsinger's devastating fumble in the 1954 Grey Cup game.

"I guess Ivy had a hunch, because he sent me in on defence on the other side from Parker. So we both had quarterbacks in there on defence in the last few moments. When Jackie picked that ball up, I was jumping up and down and begging him to run faster. I knew he had a broken bone in his foot, all wrapped up, and I was worrying that Sam [Etcheverry] might catch him.

"Funny thing, but Angelo Mosca arranged a table at a charity dinner this year. There was Sam, Hunsinger, Hal Patterson and me. It was forty-three years after the fact, and Chuck was still claiming the fumble was a forward pass. And I was still asking, 'Right, Chuck, you always throw your forward passes with two hands?' "

Faloney's other moment of unexpected glory, the Run (Eastern Division), came in the second game of the 1961 eastern final against Toronto. The Argos won the first game handily, 25-7. But Hamilton stormed back in the second game at home. They led 20-7 after sixty minutes, tying the series at 27-27.

Faloney says, "Toronto had just tried to protect their lead in the second game and we were sure we could catch them. For a few horrible minutes, I thought I had shot our chances completely. With a bit more than a minute to go, I threw an interception. I figured Henley could beat Stan Wallace, but Wallace took it away.

"They were close enough to punt for a single to win it on the first play, but Lou Agase wanted to run out the clock. They lost 7 yards on their first two plays and that meant that Dave Mann had a hell of a long punt, even for his strong leg.

"Trimble turned to me on the bench and said, 'Get in there. If you get the punt, boot it back.' So it was Don Sutherin and me in the end zone. Sutherin caught Mann's first punt 13 yards deep and kicked it back. Mann got it again and kicked it again. I caught it 3 yards deep and when I looked up, I saw the two biggest sons-of-bitches I had ever seen in my life, Toronto's tackles, bearing down on me. All I wanted to do was run it out to the 1. I stepped inside, then out, the tackles ran into each other, and everything opened up. I just ran and ran. I figured that if I didn't fall down or die, I'd score and we had it. I did score, but we didn't have it. Grant McKee had thrown an illegal block behind me. No touchdown; we're still tied. Thank God, though, we scored 4 touchdowns in overtime and won it."

Like many others, Faloney's fondness for the entire Hamilton experience has never diminished. "I know how we felt as Hamilton players. We felt that if we took care of Hamilton football, Hamilton would care of us. We always felt, this is where we want to be."

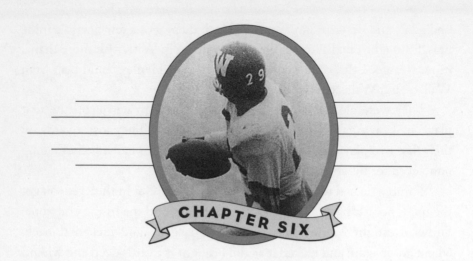

CHAPTER SIX

The Grey Fox:
Winnipeg Blue Bombers

A lone figure stalked the frozen sidelines of Winnipeg Stadium as the early twilight sapped any remnant of cheer out of the bleak October day, the hood of his parka drawn up against the chilling gusts whipping unimpeded across the open prairie. His face was in shadow, but his eyes—chill blue as a Fort Churchill ice floe, penetrating as a hayfork—shone forth, calculating, commanding, intimidating.

That lone figure—those eyes—became an emblem for late-season prairie football in Winnipeg. Following an all-star career at tight end with the Bombers, Harry Peter "Bud" Grant, "the Grey Fox," coached the team to five Grey Cups in six years—winning four—before heading south to bring glory to his home-state Minnesota Vikings.

Grant was a man of few words, but he was a very clever man. He surrounded himself with people who had the necessary coaching character-istics he lacked. The line coach, John Michels, was a fiery, chew-your-butt-off type who provided the real ass-kicking atmosphere needed to keep players focussed. The other coach, Joe Zaleski, could break the ten-sion with humour and relax the players when they were becoming too anxious or too down on themselves.

Michels once said, "Bud mostly just sits and listens. He trusts our judgement. He's like the president. Sometimes he'll offer a suggestion. And we tell him to shut up. But I'd look at a game film six times, then show it to Grant. He'd see in one viewing what it took me six to see."

Frank Rigney, who played for Grant for ten years, recalls, "Bud was one of the brightest men I've ever seen, particularly in terms of common sense. He wasn't a nuclear physicist or anything, but he knew what the situation required, and he wasn't afraid to take a chance and do whatever was necessary. Grant was a leader.

"He was a huge factor in keeping us together. One of the things Grant had going for him was his personality, which is naturally aloof and very quiet. To this day, if you don't want to talk hunting or fishing or football, there's not much left as far as he's concerned.

"When they picked the Bombers' all-time team in 1993, Grant was the coach. While we were standing on the field someone asked him, 'Bud, do you see much of the guys from the old days?' He shot back, 'Not unless they're in a goddamned duck blind.'

"He was also a cheap son of a gun. Gordie Rowland once borrowed a candy bar from him, and a year later Bud was still hounding him for his candy bar."

Before Grant took over as head coach in 1957, the Bombers' fortunes had been mixed. Back in 1935, when they were known as the Winnipegs, the team had brought the West its first Grey Cup, beating the hometown Hamilton Tigers largely on the Hall-of-Fame efforts of their diminutive halfback Fritz Hanson, who in that one game gained 300 yards in punt returns alone.

But latterly, the Bombers had led the West in Grey Cup appearances only to become the whipping boys for the Argonauts—three straight years from 1945 through '47, and again in 1950—and the Tiger-Cats, in

1953. In fact, they hadn't beaten Hamilton in twenty years. Not even the gritty heroics of Indian Jack Jacobs or the great multi-sport talent of Gerry James, who kept in shape during the off-season by playing hockey for the NHL's Toronto Maple Leafs, had been sufficient to bring home Earl Grey's teacup.

The Bombers fared no better in Grant's first year as their leader, falling 32-7 to the Ti-Cats in Toronto. But the next year their fortunes began to change. The Bombers and the Tiger-Cats were to turn the national championship into a two-team grudge match that would last the better part of a decade.

The 1958 season did not start out auspiciously. Rigney, fresh from starring at tackle with the Rose Bowl champion University of Iowa under their great head coach Forrest Evashevski, did not catch up with the Bombers until the end of training camp. "I arrived in Winnipeg on a Thursday, and Friday morning we had to fly to Montreal for an exhibition game. They beat us soundly. After the game, we got on an airplane at midnight, then got off in Toronto in the wee hours. I said, 'What are we getting off here for, changing planes or something?' Someone said, 'No, we're playing Toronto tomorrow.' I said, 'What do you mean, tomorrow? We just played yesterday.' That was my first experience with doubleheaders. In college, we played only ten games in a whole season.

The first Winnipeg win under Bud Grant was for years the best game in the history of the Grey Cup.

"Well, Toronto beat us too. So, I'd been in the country four days and we'd been beaten handily by two eastern teams who really weren't the powerhouses. I didn't know what I'd gotten myself into. I was really a bit concerned.

"But Grant was very much a taskmaster. When we got back to Winnipeg after those two losses, he got us back into full gear, hitting drills and everything else, twice a day. I've never heard of a team before or since that has done that once the exhibition season began. We started off disastrously and wound up winning the Grey Cup."

That first Winnipeg win under Grant was for years considered the best game in the history of the Grey Cup. A handful of times that afternoon the lead changed, as both teams marched up and down the Empire Stadium turf. The Bombers were down 14-0, then came back to gain and lose the lead twice before cementing it for good with 8 points in the final quarter, prevailing 35-28.

Mid-season 1958, in a loss against Calgary, Bomber Gerry James, 1957's most outstanding Canadian player, had been knocked out for the balance of the year with a broken leg, and starting quarterback Kenny Ploen suffered a strained shoulder. Jim Van Pelt, a highly touted rookie out of the University of Michigan, stepped into Ploen's cleats and promptly led the Bombers to a 43-13 victory over the Eskimos. Grant was so impressed that, when Ploen returned from injury, he left Van Pelt where he was and converted Ploen, his all-star Grey Cup quarterback of a year before, to a halfback. Initially, the move was met with skepticism.

Grant's judgement was vindicated as the multi-talented Van Pelt scored 22 points in 1958's Grey Cup game against the Ti-Cats, on 2 touchdowns (1 as a receiver on an option pass by halfback Leo Lewis), 2 field goals and 4 converts. In doing so Van Pelt surpassed Jackie Parker's Grey Cup record of 19, set two years earlier. Former Pittsburgh Steeler and Baltimore Colt fullback Charlie Shepard racked up 120 yards in 14 carries, an 8 1/2-yard average. The tone of Bomber–Ti-Cat confrontations to come was set late in the first half by Ti-Cat defender Ralph Goldston, who was ejected for slugging the Bombers' Leo Lewis in the face. "Boy, that was terrible," exclaimed Hamilton head coach Jim Trimble, commenting not on Goldston's action but on that of referee Taylor Paterson, who penalized the player. "If they're trying to ruin the game, they're doing a good job."

The next season, Grant left Van Pelt where he was and put Ploen into the defensive backfield. All Ploen did was play well enough to be voted an all-star at the position. Van Pelt continued to excel, passing for 7 touchdowns in an early season game and breaking Jack Jacobs's record. The Bombers finished the season in first place at 12-4, then again outpointed Edmonton in the western finals.

By that time, a quirk of fate in the form of a dislocated shoulder injury to Van Pelt in the second-to-last game of the 1959 regular season had made Kenny Ploen once again the Bombers' starting pivot. The scene was set for the rubber match of three consecutive annual Grey Cup match-ups between Winnipeg and Hamilton.

Anticipation was high among fans and media that this, the fiftieth Grey Cup, would be the best confrontation yet. After a pre-season game between the two teams that Hamilton won, Trimble had offered the unsolicited opinion that Van Pelt was the better Bomber quarterback, saying that he "moved the ball better" and Ploen "ran too much." Ploen and his teammates were determined to prove Trimble wrong on the field.

But although the setting for the game was new—Toronto's CNE Stadium was chosen to replace the boggy Varsity Stadium—on game day it almost seemed as if groundskeepers had gone out of their way to transport the Bloor Street quagmire to the new venue. The sloppy turf stymied both offences and the teams slithered to a 3-1 Bomber lead at halftime. Propelled by Charlie Shepard's booming punts and quick kicks, which together accounted for 4 singles on the day, the Bombers established a territorial advantage in the second half. Yet, at the end of the third quarter, they trailed 7-3. Somehow, in the final fifteen minutes, they found enough footing to score a couple of touchdowns, one on a 2-yard plunge by Shepard and another on a 35-yard pass and run from Ploen to Pitts. That was good enough for a 21-7 victory over the Ti-Cats, who were unable to score a single touchdown all day.

The second win affirmed that the 1958 Cup had been no fluke, and a Bomber dynasty was born. The team finished first in the West five straight years, from 1958 through 1962. Over that span they appeared in four Grey Cups, missing only in 1960 when they were tripped up in the western final by the Edmonton Eskimos.

Like any dynasty in sports, they relied in part on a system and in part on their players. Grant used to say, "There are no new plays in football. We just steal ones that have already been created." He was a master of adaptation, finding a play or a strategy that someone else had used successfully and making it fit with the personnel he had on hand.

"One of Bud's greatest attributes," says Ken Ploen today, "was his ability to recognize talent *and* what to do with it. He kept who he wanted and cut who he wanted, and sometimes you'd wonder, at the time, about the choices that he made. But I think he recognized that, at the pro level, everybody's got talent. It's how you put a team together—the chemistry, the camaraderie, that makes the difference."

Grant took the attitude that he was going to keep the best twelve players on either side of the ball. Not necessarily the best tackle or the best end or the best running back, but the best twelve men who could play the game, and then match them to a position. The way he had swapped and switched Ploen and Van Pelt on the road to two consecutive Grey Cup victories had shown that Grant's strategy was an effective one.

In training camp before the 1958 season, there were four offensive tackles but only two spots available. Bob Hobert, a Rhodes scholar from the University of Minnesota, took one spot, while rookie Frank Rigney and veteran Stavros Canakes contested the second. Canakes had been Bud Grant's roommate all through the time Grant played in Winnipeg, yet ultimately Grant cut him to make room for Rigney. Here was a man unafraid of tough decisions. From that point on, for years, Canakes refused to speak to his old pal. Little did he know that the opportune phone call he received days after being cut, offering him a coaching job in another city, was no coincidence. Grant had made a call of his own, recommending Canakes for the job.

The players Grant kept were among the best in football, anywhere. For the long term, his quarterback of choice was Kenny Ploen. Ploen, who hailed from Lost Nation, Iowa, and had led the University of Iowa to Rose Bowl victory in 1957, established himself as the Bombers' field general. Says Rigney, "Kenny was great. Ploen is a German name, and believe me, Kenny has some of the characteristics you expect of the German nationality. He was very dogmatic, very much a leader. Nobody spoke back to him, and if you were making suggestions in the huddle and they weren't welcome, you were told to shut up and do your job."

Ploen was a good example of Grant basing his player selection on individuals who were the best football players, not the most spectacular athletes. Rigney, who blocked for Ploen for all but one of his years at quarterback, offers this assessment: "Kenny had a great sense of what it takes to win. He was very bright, was actually a fairly good runner, and he was a good passer in that he could get the ball there. It didn't always look pretty. But he knew how to pick a defence apart."

Ploen never led the league in completions or passing yardage, the way that Jack Jacobs had or that Dieter Brock, or even Don Jonas, would later do. Only once, in 1965, was he voted the top quarterback in Canada. His career statistics are not that impressive. All Ken Ploen did was win ball games. All he did was lead his team to Grey Cup victories—three of them.

In the backfield, Ploen handed off to a series of solid performers: Gerry James, Charlie Shepard, Dave Raimey, to name only a few. Probably the best all-round running back among a stellar collection was Leo Lewis. Lewis, a six-time all-star, was a glider who would never run over a defender. Instead, he would find a way to slip around him. "I just loved to watch him run," remembers Ploen. "He never looked fast, but nobody could catch him, because he had such great acceleration and leg strength." Although he never led the league in rushing yardage, Lewis tallied more than 1,000 yards twice, in 1958 and 1961, averaging better than 7 yards each time he carried the ball. He was also a reliable receiver and could pass the ball accurately on the option play. His 5,444 total career yards on kickoff returns is still a league record.

At either end of his offensive line, Ploen had at his disposal two constants: Ernie Pitts and Farrell Funston. Pitts played right end throughout Ploen's eleven-year career, doubling much of the time at defensive back as well. Funston consistently held down the left side over his nine-year career. Both were exceptional players, honoured as all-stars. Pitts ran patterns so accurate Ploen seldom had to look for him; he knew precisely where Pitts would be. And Pitts was fast. Hitting his stride going deep on a flag or post pattern, he was uncatchable. "I can remember my first day in camp, out at the old Canada Packers practice field," recalls Ploen. "I saw a player who seemed to be just jogging along across the field—but fast—and I said, 'Wow, who is that?' because his speed seemed so effortless." The sure-handed Funston was tough enough to take the punishment dealt out by linebackers and defensive backs on shorter patterns. But great as their on-field accomplishments were, Pitts and Funston were equally notorious for their extra-curricular behaviour.

Pitts was quite the ladies' man, and he paid the ultimate price for it:

he was shot dead by his jealous wife. Frank Rigney tells a story of being approached by a waiter in a Vancouver bar in the spring of 1997; the waiter asked Rigney if he might have known Ernie Pitts. Rigney allowed that he had known Pitts well. The waiter then related that, raised by adoptive parents, he had recently sought out his birth mother. When he contacted her, she told him his father had been Pitts. He said she had added, "Don't be shocked, as you travel around Canada, if you find that you have a number of half-brothers and half-sisters."

Funston was a wild man, the jokester on the team. After practice, the players would usually stop in for a beer or two at their favourite hangout, the Swinging Gate, on the west side of Main Street near Broadway, hard by the railway station. One night, Funston and Wayne "Whisky" Dennis grew tired of betting for beers on their dart games, so they faced off for higher stakes. The loser had to walk—not run—naked down Portage Avenue in downtown Winnipeg. Dennis lost. With Funston driving alongside him, Dennis's clothes on the car's front seat, Dennis started off, walking quickly at first. But Dennis was never noted for his speed, and he soon slowed to a saunter, naked as a jaybird. It was around suppertime. There were plenty of people on the sidewalk, and Funston kept flashing the headlights on and off, sounding the horn so that nobody could miss what was going on. Hints Rigney, "That was one of the tamer things those two got up to."

Pitts was fast. Hitting his stride deep on a flag or post pattern, he was uncatchable.

With Funston and Pitts running off in all directions mystifying defenders, the core protection for Ploen was provided by a solid, enduring, stay-at-home offensive middle. For years, his veteran offensive line kept the occasionally fragile Ploen intact. "Kenny had a crushed-in chest," recalls Rigney, "and every time he got hit by one of the defensive linemen, it sounded like he would never get up. We tried to avoid him getting hit, but that didn't always work."

Some players came and went, but the Winnipeg Blue Bombers offensive front line of the late 1950s to '60s was remarkable for its collective longevity. Pitts played for thirteen years; Funston for eight. Rigney at left tackle lasted ten years; Winnipegger Cornell Piper at left and then right guard, eleven. Piper was succeeded on the left by Sherwyn Thorson, the NCAA heavyweight wrestling champion at Iowa, who stayed seven years in Winnipeg, as, on the right side of the line, did Ed Kotowich, who played his junior football with the Winnipeg Junior Rods. Winnipeg-born George Druxman anchored the centre for nine.

On the defensive side, too, the Bombers' success was sustained by a hardy core of veterans. Herb Gray played eleven years, including five years as a western all-star at end. Seven-time western all-star tackle Buddy Tinsley lasted eleven years as well. Steve Patrick anchored the defence for thirteen years, from 1952 to 1964, and was an all-star at middle guard behind the five-man front line of the Bombers' eagle defence in 1958 and 1959. Gordie Rowland for eleven years, Norm Rauhaus for twelve and Roger Savoie for fifteen—all-stars all at one time in their careers—contributed mightily to the Bombers' enduring success. Patrick, Rauhaus, Tinsley and Savoie were Manitoba boys. "Having played there for three years before he took over as coach, Bud recognized that he had a number of talented Canadians," notes Ploen, "and he brought in imports to build around them."

With long service came comradeship, communication, trust and knowledge about teammates' tendencies. In a Bombers game there would be a constant verbal flow, in the players' own private lingo, about opponents' moves or their own blocking assignments. If one of them went down because of injury, the others could shift around temporarily, because each knew so well what the others were doing.

Many of the Bombers stayed on in Winnipeg after the season ended, settling into business and family life. To Americans from the warmer states, the winters were a bit of a shock. Rigney recalls that the first winter he, his wife and baby son spent there, the temperature never rose above −25 degrees the whole month of January. But the team stuck together, even in the off-season. One year, a basketball team Grant, Funston, Ploen, Rigney, Nick Miller and some other players assembled to help them keep in shape came within two points of winning the Canadian championships.

The gel that held them all together was, without question, Bud Grant. Rigney relates a telling example of the loyalty given to Grant by the Bombers' all-star defensive end Herb Gray. In the early part of the season, once the NFL teams started cutting down their rosters, the Bombers' management would fly in some of the more promising discards for a trial. Grant would always call upon Gray to get into full-dress uniform and pads to test the new players' mettle. "He'd beat the hell out of them to see if they wanted to play," says Rigney. Of course, Gray would be taking some hard shots in return. "And he always bitched about it," recalls Rigney. "He'd say, 'I'll never do that again,' and then Grant would look at him and say, 'Herb, I need you in full uniform again tomorrow,' and Herbie would say 'Okay, coach!'"

Player loyalty was not based on any special privileges Grant extended to them. In late-season games played on the blasted frozen prairie, no matter how low the mercury descended, Grant would never allow his players the luxury of wearing long underwear or gloves, nor would he let the equipment men provide hot-air blowers on the sidelines. He reasoned that there was only one place and one way the players should be keeping warm: on the field, running and hitting.

Grant may have been the lodestone, but part of the magnetism he fostered was the sense of belonging, of team spirit over individualism. "I remember when Hal Ledyard first came in as a backup quarterback, he was kind of a cocky individual," says Ploen. "Well, that was one thing you just couldn't get away with for long on the Bombers. For a team meeting before an exhibition game against Ottawa, a bunch of us got together— Grant was in on it, too—and made up signs that read things like 'To Hal and back' and 'To hell with Hal.' When he came into the room, we all held them up. It didn't take him long after that to come around."

In an age when eastern and western teams rarely played each other except in pre-season and playoffs (a partial interlocking schedule was not in place until 1961), CFL players knew their opposing numbers nearly as well as their teammates. Says Rigney, "One guy I really got to know was Roger Nelson, who played opposite me for Edmonton. One year we played against each other seven times, pre-season, regular season and playoffs. So Roger and I would talk about our families, as much as anything."

One team the Bombers saw a lot of over those years was, of course, the Hamilton Tiger-Cats. Rigney offers an insight into the lineplay, the trench warfare that often turned the tide when the two teams did battle.

"Probably the best all-around lineman that I played against was John Barrow. With Barrow, it was a guessing game. When John really wanted to come after you on pass protection, for example, you couldn't let him get up a head of steam. You had to stick him and stop him right there, and then, because he was so quick, you had to get away from him and set up for the next move, because he had good feet. And if you allow a guy full momentum who's got good feet, he's going to get past you.

"Sometimes he'd play placid, hang back like he wasn't coming at all, then all of a sudden, boom, he'd go to the inside. He was a guy you had to be very wary of all the time because he had all the moves.

"Angelo Mosca was kind of a bull in a china shop. Although he was bigger and stonger than John, I didn't think he was nearly as good a football player.

"I also went up against Billy Ray Locklin at defensive end. On some plays I would slide out and block on him, and he was tough. He was big and strong and came hard every play. Although it's easier to block a guy who's a bull, you do take a beating because he was big and strong."

Hamilton and Winnipeg had met in the Grey Cup classic four times over the course of the 1950s, winning twice apiece. At the start of the 1960 season, every expectation had it that they would meet again that November. But Hamilton stumbled out of the blocks and slumped to a 4-10 season. Winnipeg, on the other hand, finished at 14-2, the best record it would ever attain under Grant. Van Pelt had been lost to a three-year Air Force service commitment that would cut short his athletic career. Under Ploen, the Bomber offence tallied 453 points—the best anyone had done since the Eskimos in their heyday—and the defence held opponents to a stingy 239 points, second best in the league. In the western final series, they handled Edmonton 22-16 in the opener, but then the Eskimo defence—which had allowed only 225 points over the regular season, easily the league's least generous defence—took over, holding the Bombers to a total of 7 points over the final two games. The Esks, however, forgot that you also have to *score* points to win ball games and lost 16-6 to Ottawa in the national final.

The next year it was business as usual for the Bombers and the Ti-Cats, as Winnipeg set out to reclaim the Grey Cup for the West, while

Hamilton sought to overcome their blue-and-gold nemesis. Fan interest was extreme. Mr. Justice Ruttan of the Ontario Assize Court cancelled a Saturday afternoon session of a stock fraud hearing so members of the jury (and, more than likely, Judge Ruttan), could watch the game, which was held in Toronto. The match was an even one, so even, in fact, that, for the first time in more than half a century of Grey Cup history, it took more than sixty minutes to determine the result.

One team the Bombers saw a lot of over those years was the Hamilton Ti-Cats.

The Ti-Cats had rolled to a 14-4 lead with less than twenty minutes left in the game. But the Bombers refused to abandon their game plan, which relied on the ground game and a slow but steady approach. On the day, they amassed 268 net yards rushing to the Ti-Cats' paltry total of 25. Ploen completed only twelve passes but made them count, including a key outlet pass to Farrell Funston on second down and 30 that set up Gerry James's game-tying touchdown. At the end of regulation play, the teams were even at 14-14.

They played one scoreless ten-minute overtime period. Then, less than three minutes into the second half of overtime, Ploen scrambled out of the pocket and rambled 18 yards for what stood up as the winning touchdown. The Bombers held the Ti-Cats scoreless the rest of the way to win 21-14.

The following season, the teams took the field for what would become one of the strangest encounters in football, immortalized as the "Fog Bowl." An unseasonable warm spell caused an impenetrable fog bank to drift ashore from Lake Ontario, enveloping CNE Stadium as the game progressed. Although the players and coaches at field level could see enough to get by, the paying customers in the grandstands and the television audience at home were not as fortunate. In a moment of candour, CBC broadcaster Johnny Esaw confessed over the air, "I really don't know what's going on down there."

"You could see the guy you were blocking," says Rigney. "There was a ceiling of probably eight or ten feet—it was like a big cloud hanging over us. It affected the passing game; you just couldn't do it. And obviously, if you can't do that, they're going to stop the running game. When we punted, we'd just go like hell and look for the guy looking for the ball."

CFL officials huddled periodically to debate whether to allow the game to continue. Fans in the higher reaches of the stadium, amused at first, began to turn surly. Finally, with less than ten minutes to play in the fourth quarter and Winnipeg leading 28-27, CFL commissioner Sydney Halter called the game. "We were a little surprised when they called us over to the sidelines and suspended play," remembers Ploen. "And we were a lot more surprised when they told us they were postponing it until the next day. When they called the game on Saturday, we were second and long. So, we had twenty-four hours to decide on the next play. It didn't do us any good, though, because we failed to convert it."

The Bomber players found themselves in a quandary. It was Saturday night, the night of the Grey Cup, traditionally the time for the party of the year. By all rights they ought to be out on the town, either celebrating another victory or washing away a defeat. Yet here they were, with a game—or at least part of a game—to play the next day. "After the game was called off for the day," Rigney recalls, "everybody was wondering what sort of curfew there would be. Herb Gray and I were the two captains. Grant said to Herbie and me, 'Gentlemen, I have nothing to say to you. You have ten minutes to play and a lifetime to think about it. So, I'd like to ask you guys to hold a team meeting and decide what you want to do about it.' Well, of course, he had put the onus straight on us. We set our own curfews, and everybody complied with them."

The next day, they and their Tiger-Cat counterparts had another shock to their routine. The day after a game is usually a time for nursing injuries ignored during the heat of battle. Aches and pains, and worse, emerge from the post-game euphoria. The next day, a team's training room is a place players go to seek the ministrations of the medical staff, not pre-game preparation. Says Rigney, "It was a scary locker room. Guys were screaming in pain as they were getting shot up with painkillers."

So, on a damp, cool but clear Sunday afternoon, two stiff, sore groups of players went through the motions for the remaining nine minutes and twenty-nine seconds without affecting the final result. At a public victory ceremony held the next day at the Winnipeg Arena, 5,000 loyal fans cheered as a tiger skin was laid at Bud Grant's feet. Uncustomarily moved, Grant confessed, "For the first time in the last couple of weeks I'm at a loss for words."

Neither Grant nor anyone else knew that this would be his last opportunity to savour Grey Cup victory. Only once more, in 1965, would his Bombers make the national final. Speaking at the annual Grey Cup dinner in 1965, Philip Givens, mayor of the host city of Toronto, said, "This is a night when you can feel unity in Canada," thereby proving that he was not particularly knowledgeable about Canadian football. On the gridiron, national unity was nowhere to be found. This was the sixth such meeting between the Ti-Cats and the Bombers. The Ti-Cats, unsuccessful against Winnipeg since 1957, were determined to break the Bomber jinx. The Bombers, absent from the annual classic for two years, were determined to reclaim their national title.

But Mother Nature intervened to quash what ought to have been a splendid contest. Gale force winds off Lake Ontario blew away any chance Bud Grant might have for one last victory.

Grant left after the 1966 season to coach the NFL Vikings. Five years later, he would tell *Weekend Magazine* reporter Paul Rimstead, "Football in Canada, in the West anyway, can't be improved on as entertainment. The public doesn't realize how good the CFL is."

Many of the veteran players quit soon after Grant left town for good. Says Rigney, "It just wasn't fun any more." The Bombers, without Grant, would slide to the bottom of the Western Conference for the balance of the sixties, and would not return to the Grey Cup until their 1984 win under Don Matthews.

With the passing of Grant and his veterans came the beginning of the end, not just of Bomber greatness but of a whole style of play. "The game was slower in those days," says Rigney. "We used to run plays with counter crisscross. The quarterback would turn, hand to one halfback. The other halfback would take a step the wrong way, then come back, and take the ball from the other halfback. Nowadays, I'm not sure you could keep those linemen and linebackers out of there long enough to do that. It certainly would be only an occasional play. When we ran it, we ran it a lot. And of course we faked it, and we ran pass patterns off it.

There was maybe a little more ball deception in those days. Defences weren't as good, didn't react as quickly as they do now.

"In the days that I played, the difference in playing calibre between the CFL and the NFL was not that great. In college, for league or all-star games, I roomed with Ray Nitschke, I played with Alex Karras and against players like Paul Hornung and Jerry Kramer, who went on to win under Vince Lombardi in Green Bay. They were good, there's no question about it. But they weren't that much better than we were. And the pay scale wasn't that much different, especially for linemen. My initial contract was $8,000 plus a $500 signing bonus. I was told it was the same money Big Daddy Lipscomb was getting with the Baltimore Colts. And the Canadian dollar was worth 108 cents U.S. then."

Like their counterparts in Hamilton, the Winnipeg Blue Bombers under Bud Grant had earned success by practising homespun virtues such as patience and hard work, loyalty and pride. A system was in place, a winning formula, but it was adapted to suit the strengths of the best players, the best *football* talent, the Bombers could acquire. The Winnipeg fans offered the team their loyalty in return. That's Winnipeg.

By way of an example of the warm, generous community spirit that inhabits the Manitoba capital, Rigney relates a story about Kenny Ploen. After his playing days were over, Ploen remained with his family in Winnipeg. Thirty years later, he is still there. Ploen sold his house in the fall of 1996, but the deal didn't close until April 30 the next year. As it turned out, May 1 was the day the Red River peaked during the great flood of 1997. Days before, even though the deal was done, Ploen ordered in sandbags to protect what would soon no longer be his property. On the Saturday night, trucks dropped off 7,200 sandbags in front of the house. By nine-thirty the next morning, there were 150 to 175 people outside, helping to sandbag. "It reminded me of growing up in Iowa, when the farmers would get together to thresh each other's grain," says Ploen when asked about the incident.

"That's a typical Winnipeg attitude," says Rigney. "It's a great city that way."

Previous page: A meteoric temperament kept the brilliant Cookie Gilchrist (#21) from realizing his full potential. CFHF

Head coaches create their own personal style in their struggle to motivate their teams to victory. *Top left:* Quietly inspirational, Bud Grant (with Ken Ploen) forged loyalty and a winning desire over

his decade in Winnipeg. CANAPRESS PHOTO SERVICE

Bottom left: Nervous and obsessive, Frank Clair—"The Professor"—led the Argos and Rough Riders to five Grey Cups. BRIAN KENT/VANCOUVER SUN

Above: Critical and controlling, the Alouettes' Perry Moss *(left)* and his fiery

assistant Leo Cahill *(right)* alienated star
quarterback Sam Etcheverry (#14). CFHF

Inset right: Screening game films to scout
opponents—illegal when the era began—
helped Dave Skrien *(centre)* and assistants Jim Champion *(left)* and Frank
Johnston bring B.C. Lions a Grey Cup.
THE PROVINCE

Canadian football is a physical game. Those who excel at it are those who sacrifice their bodies in a supreme effort to make the catch, to make the diving tackle, to gain that extra yard.

Left: Hamilton's Garney Henley hangs on to the ball while a Montreal defender cuts his feet out from under him. CFHF

Below: Argos' superstar Dick Shatto (with ball) looks to gain even more yardage despite being wrapped up by a Ti-Cat tackler. CFHF

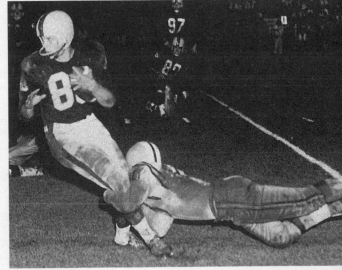

Trades were a fact of football life, then as now, even for the best players. Being traded comes as a blow, but it can also energize a career.

Above: The indomitable Ron Lancaster (#16), caught in a battle with Russ Jackson for the Ottawa starting quarterback's job, took the West by storm when he was traded to Saskatchewan. He went on to become the most prolific passer in Canadian football history. CFHF

Right: Moving from Edmonton to Hamilton didn't faze Tommy Joe Coffey. He won all-Canadian honours at offensive end four years with the Eskimos and three years with the Ti-Cats. CFHF

From the first workout of training camp to the final whistle of the season, it all comes down to a quest for the silverware.

Right: Norm Fieldgate, shown in 1962 with his arm around a more tangible reward, was honoured in 1978 when the Western Conference Trophy for outstanding defensive player was renamed the Norm Fieldgate Trophy. BRIAN KENT/VANCOUVER SUN

Inset: The best in the league in 1963 were the Rough Riders' Russ Jackson *(left)*, named outstanding player and outstanding Canadian, and outstanding lineman Tom Brown of the B.C. Lions. VANCOUVER SUN

Below: With a tip of his hat, Ti-Cats quarterback Bernie Faloney salutes Hamilton's 1963 triumph. THE PROVINCE

Left: Saskatchewan veteran lineman Ron Atchison, a product of Saskatoon junior football, waited fifteen seasons to drink deeply from the Grey Cup. He finally got his chance, along with teammates Larry Dumelie and Jack Abendschan, after the Riders' long-awaited 1966 victory over Ottawa. BRIAN KENT/ VANCOUVER SUN

Below: The game was viewed across Canada nationally on that novelty, colour television. CFHF

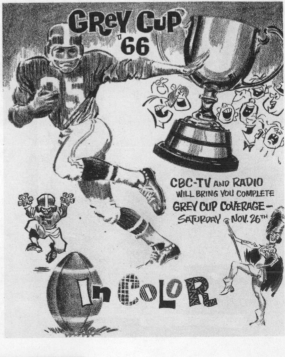

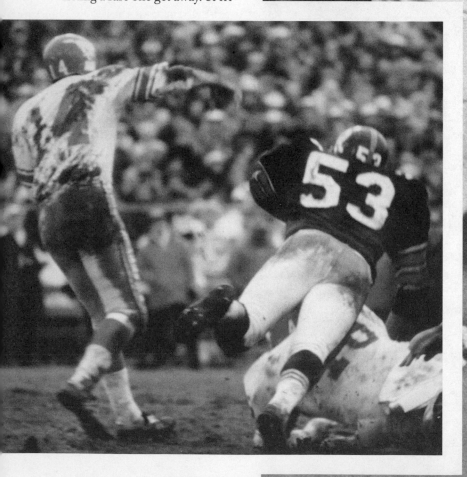

Dormant for nearly two decades, the Calgary Stampeders closed out the era with a trio of Grey Cup appearances. The engine of Calgary's renewed success was the play of quarterback Peter Liske (*below:* #14), named Canada's outstanding player in 1967, and receiver Terry Evanshen, the league's outstanding Canadian in 1967 and '71, shown here *(right)* letting a rare one get away. CFHF

Above: Twice Calgary was turned
back: in 1968 by Ottawa under
Russ Jackson; and in 1970 by
Sonny Wade and the Montreal
Alouettes. It was not until
1971, led by Liske's former
backup, Jerry Keeling (#10), that
the Stamps tasted from the
Cup. CFHF

Right: The epitome of a
Canadian sporting hero, Russ
Jackson conducted himself with
dignity, dedication, intelligence
and a consuming competitive
nature to shower himself with
personal honours and lead his
Ottawa Rough Riders to
three Grey Cups. CFHF

Not once since the 1969 Grey Cup has a Canadian
starting quarterback raised the victor's trophy above
his head. Will it ever happen again? Or was the
postwar quarter-century a unique time when myth
and legend converged upon the gridiron to produce
Canadian—*truly* Canadian—football? CFHF

CHAPTER SEVEN

Wet and Wild:
British Columbia Lions

The British Columbia Lions came to Canadian football like an unwanted child—runty, squalling, colicky. Small wonder, considering that the infant franchise was conceived over drinks in an upstairs nightclub one night in 1951. The child was born in 1954. It was a long and hard labour.

On that 1951 night, two Vancouver sportsmen, Ken Stauffer and Tiny Rader, were sipping Scotch in Stauffer's Arctic Club, a popular Pender Street bistro where soft jazz was played by the brilliant young pianist Chris Gage and bar drinks were three for a dollar. Stauffer and Rader, the owner of Love's Cafe, a late-night Granville Street restaurant where waiters wore floor-length butcher aprons, were discussing Andy Lytle's thumbsucker. Lytle was a well-read Vancouver sports columnist. It being a time of scant legitimate sports news, Lytle had taken the columnist's last resort, wherein the writer sucks his thumb, ponders deep and composes an essay, usually beginning with the words, "Isn't it about time that . . ." or perhaps "It beats me why . . ."

Lytle's column expressed outrage that Vancouver, the third biggest city in Canada, was shut out by Canadian football. Four smaller prairie cities had teams. Sarnia, for cryin' out loud, had a team in the Ontario Rugby Football Union. Why not Vancouver?

Why not, indeed, said Stauffer and Rader. They took that question to the movers and shakers around town, and Orville Burke and Rader carried it, at their own expense, to the 1951 Western Interprovincial Football Union (WIFU) meeting on the prairies, where they applied for a franchise. They were not welcomed warmly, nor was their proposal. They were told to come back the following year with a $25,000 good-faith bond and they might be taken seriously.

Back in Vancouver, a very loose coalition of like-minded men gathered in the Vancouver *Province* sports department. The crowd was so large and so noisy that the editor-in-chief bellowed he couldn't get a bloody paper out with all those bloody strangers milling around. The crowd moved down the street to the Boilermakers' Union hall. There the decision was made to plunge ahead, whatever it took, and a ten-man working committee was formed. A fedora was passed and $17.50 in silver was collected. Since the rent on the hall was $15, the fledgling Vancouver Football Club was left with a treasury of $2.50 in seed money.

Three committee members, president Art Mercer, Bill Ralston and Dr. Whit Matthews, the dean of pharmacy at the University of B.C. and a former Canadian Rugby Union president, attended the 1952 WIFU meeting in Regina, armed with the required $25,000 note. Calgary and Edmonton voted to let Vancouver in, Winnipeg and Regina voted against, and league president Fred Wilson of Winnipeg, with the deciding ballot, voted against. The delegates came home again, discouraged but not defeated.

They were right to be optimistic. A slow-gathering break was about to come Vancouver's way from across an ocean.

A year earlier, Vancouver *Sun* sports editor Erwin Swangard, reading wire copy, had seen a story that said applications for host city for the 1954 British Empire Games would be accepted at the 1950 games in Auckland. It was after midnight, but Swangard phoned Vancouver mayor Fred Hume, woke him up, read him the story and said, "We're going to apply." Hume mumbled assent and went back to sleep. Swangard went to Auckland and lobbied vigorously, and in 1953 Vancouver was announced as host of the 1954 games. Years later, Swangard told columnist Archie McDonald how Vancouver got the BEG. "We lied like hell," said Swangard. "We lied about facilities we didn't have."

So now, when Vancouver Football Club delegates went to their third straight WIFU meeting in January 1953, they not only had a bank account to deal, they had a blueprint for the biggest stadium in Canada. This time they got conditional acceptance. They would receive a franchise on completion of a stadium with a minimum of 15,000 seats; in addition, they must sell 11,000 season tickets, and they must guarantee any extra expenses to prairie teams travelling to the coast.

The Lions were in. They had money to operate, a canny manager-coach and the biggest playpen in the country.

A massive ticket drive was undertaken. An eight-game package for covered seats could be bought for $28.50, five bucks down, five months to pay the balance. Club memberships, carrying voting rights on major decisions, were sold for $20. One purchaser in suburban White Rock bought ninety-two season tickets. Eight kids bought sixteen, borrowing the money from a credit union, pledging to repay it at a dollar a week. In two weeks, 7,000 season tickets sold.

So there was money in the bank and the club had not had to borrow a penny. As bulldozers were levelling a miniature golf course out on East Hastings for the stadium, the next element was addressed: a genius to run the show. The call went out to Toronto, to Annis Stukus, who was back with the Toronto *Star* after having restored football life in Edmonton.

Looking back on it from the present day, Stukus says, "The first person to contact me was Art Mercer and I said no, that I had had enough of football. But I did promise to help, so I sent them a twenty-page paper that I labelled 'How to Start a Football Team from Scratch and Not Lose Money.' They would hold these directors' meetings and study my paper and then they'd get on the phone. That meant I was getting the calls at 3:00 a.m. Toronto time. They were killing me. So I agreed to come out for a meeting at the end of February.

"The day I left Toronto, it was cold and miserable and slushy. I had never been to Vancouver before. Now, these bastards drive me down Granville Street, through Stanley Park, down around English Bay and put me up on the beach at the Sylvia Hotel for three days of beautiful sunshine. I had never seen such beauty, the mountains, the ocean, the beaches. I phoned Doris in Toronto and said, 'Now I know why God built the Rocky Mountains—to hide Eden from us Torontonians.' I was hooked. One of my best friends, Ted Reeve, had warned me in the Toronto Press Club, 'Stuke, I know those western fish-eaters. Even you can't sell football out there.' But I signed on anyway, general manager and coach. I guess I just can't resist impossible challenges. If I'd been born a lot earlier, they would probably have sent me out on one of the Crusades."

Empire Stadium was completed on time, with 25,000 plank seats, 11,000 of them under cover. The City of Vancouver (Mayor Hume was the football club's honorary president) and the provincial and federal governments kicked in $200,000 each, a bond issue raised $750,000, and the stadium was completed for $1,371,846.21.

When the club was officially welcomed into the league, it was still a tepid greeting. Calgary and Edmonton approved wholeheartedly; Saskatchewan expressed reservations but went along. Winnipeg voted against, convinced that with 25,000 seats for sale and a 550,000 population, Vancouver could buy a winner every year and dominate the league until the end of time.

But the Lions were in. They had money to operate, a canny manager-coach with a three-year contract (at $10,000, $11,000 and $12,000), and the biggest playpen in the country. The club operated out of a small walk-up office on Hastings Street where the club's first salaried employee, Vida Scott, was in charge. She supplied her own desk and chair. A sympathetic storekeeper donated a hot plate and a floor lamp. On cold days in the unheated office, Vida put the hot plate under her chair. Stukus rarely came to the office; he was out every day selling tickets and talking up football. The late Dick Beddoes, a former Vancouver *Sun* columnist, wrote that Stukus "would give a 40-minute talk to three people under a lamp-post." Before a player had been signed, the Lions had 3,300 dues-paying members and 8,500 season ticket holders.

The next thing was putting a team together. In his first two years in Edmonton, Stukus had stolen a full starting roster from the Argos, Ottawa and Hamilton combined. Some eastern general managers felt Stukus should have been required to wear a skull-and-crossbones logo on his coaching cap. He still claims that he recruited twenty-four of the Edmonton players Pop Ivy took into the 1954 Grey Cup game.

It wouldn't be that easy in Vancouver. Stukus organized coaching clinics and tryout camps and formed a development team called the Vancouver Cubs, all-Canadian, which played a series of exhibition games around the Pacific Northwest. He even invited world champion weight-lifter Doug Hepburn and internationally rated rugby player George Puil to tryout camp. It generated great publicity.

But the first genuine star Stukus landed was a steal. For $15,000 a year and a two-year no-cut guarantee, Stukus signed Arnie Weinmeister, a great two-way lineman with the New York Giants, now a member of the NFL Hall of Fame. Besides his undoubted talent—New York columnist Red Smith once described Weinmeister after a game played on a muddy field, the front of his white sweater black with mud but with not a spot on his back—Weinmeister had been born in Saskatchewan. He would qual-ify as a Canadian. Weinmeister was still under contract to the Giants, who filed an injunction, but a King County superior court judge in Seattle ruled that the lineman was free to play for Vancouver. The week of Weinmeister's signing, the club sold 4,000 season tickets. The Lions also had to win court approval to sign both Laurie Niemi, a Washington Redskins guard, and Philadelphia Eagles fullback Al Pollard, a punishing runner who had been discharged from West Point after an examination-cribbing scandal. Stukus never did get the quarterback he wanted, Lindy Berry, who had played well in Edmonton but married wealth and lost his zest for football. Instead he brought in rookie John Mazur, a Notre Dame graduate, and second-year pro Gerry Tuttle.

As manager-coach for the Lions, Stukus found he had to deal with the opinions and ideas of twenty-nine directors, only one less than the thirty who had driven him to distraction and back to the newspaper business when he was in Edmonton. They were a hard-drinking bunch, many of those directors. But most of them lapsed into sobriety long enough to take care of business. They had worked themselves to the bone hunting and bagging the franchise. They had sold tickets, often door-to-door. They had earned a moral stake in the team, they were conscientous boosters, but there were so many of them that they tended to split off into factions. That would be a continuing problem until 1961, when outsiders had to be called in to straighten out the structure.

Stukus says today, "I told the directors I would need a $400,000 operating budget for the first year. Five directors quit on the spot. A week later I went back to them and said I needed another $40,000 for halftime shows. I said, 'Ignore what I'm telling the press and the public. We won't win a game this year so I want to give the fans a $5,000 halftime show every night.' Two more directors quit that night. They really thought I was going to bankrupt the team, and they didn't want to be responsible."

And then it was time to play football. The Lions played two exhibition games at home, against Montreal and Hamilton. They drew 29,000 to the two games, scoring no points, but showing defensive potential by holding Hamilton to -17 yards on the ground. The Lions found that the enormously successful British Empire Games, which had ended one day before the exhibition game with Montreal, had left the playing field in appalling shape—torn turf, poor drainage, treacherous footing. The restoration process was slow. In one of the league games that followed, a descending punt hit the turf and stuck, point first, like a javelin. The Lions bought a clear plastic tarpaulin to spread over the field but it formed a vacuum; gasping worms were drawn to the surface, and clouds of seagulls pecked the cover to shreds to get at them.

A Lions director, Jack LaBelle, had coined the team slogan, "The Lions Will Roar in '54." After a few tentative mews in the exhibition games, it was time to see if this cat could bellow for real.

The very first play of their very first league game, August 28, 1954, said they could roar, but only in pain. On their first offensive play, quarterback Mazur, in the beloved-by-Stukus single-wing formation, took the snap from centre Gil Steer, pivoted smartly and handed off to fullback Pollard. Unfortunately Mazur drilled the ball right between Pollard's eyes. Surprisingly, though, the Lions held a 6-5 lead in the fourth quarter, thanks to By Bailey's first-ever B.C. touchdown. But Gerry James kicked a field goal with four minutes left and Winnipeg stole it, 8-6.

It was to be a year of wonderfully creative losing.

Midseason, the Lions were nursing a 6-0 lead over Edmonton and lining up for a punt. The snap went twenty feet over kicker Don Lord's head. Edmonton recovered, scored. It was 6-6. It went to 12-6, and game to Edmonton, when a B.C. punt receiver caught a punt at the back of his end zone, decided to kick it back out and did, all the way to the B.C. 1-yard line. Another Lions punt receiver, on orders to ground the ball and give up a point, threw a wide lateral in the end zone, right into the hands of the Winnipeg punter, Jack Jacobs.

The Lions did win one game that first season, against Calgary, and the loss cost the Stampeders a playoff spot. With Calgary ahead 4-3, the Lions were third and goal on the Calgary 1. The short snap went over Mazur's head, but he continued with a fake handoff to Pollard. The Calgary defence piled en masse on Pollard. Back a few yards, Bailey picked up the overlooked ball and slogged into the end zone. Piece of cake. The Lions had their first victory. Delirious fans tore down the goalposts and slivers were sold for twenty-five cents under the Birk's clock on Granville Street that night.

In the last quarter of the final game of the season, fog blanketed the field. The officials were about to call the game, with Saskatchewan ahead, when Stukus relayed a message to the public address announcer. He asked the fans to exhale as hard as they could. It didn't work. Another loss, but nice try.

Stukus looks back and says, "They never had a chance that year, but they never gave up. If we'd have had any kind of offence, we might have won seven games instead of one. I knew early on that we were in trouble because Mazur's body was here but his head was back at Notre Dame. I pulled him out one night and told him he had to start throwing the ball. He told me, 'Coach Leahy says you should never throw the ball inside the 20.' I didn't throttle him. I said, 'Kid, that was college. This is the pros. And this is Coach Stukus saying that if you don't start throwing the ball I'm coming out there in my civvies to replace you.'"

The other Lions quarterback, Tuttle, broke his foot in the third game of the season. He tried gamely, if briefly, to play with the broken foot in a cast and a split shoe. The one-footed quarterback seemed to set a trend of physical deprivation for the B.C. team that would be repeated in future years with a one-eyed quarterback (Bob Schloredt), a quarterback with gimpy knees (Joe Kapp), a receiver with one kidney (Sonny Homer) and a one-armed general manager (Denny Veitch).

Despite the miserable season on the field, the Lions drew 135,983 spectators that first year and finished with a profit of $58,763 on an operating budget (for players, coaches and training) of $216,264.54. That performance got Stukus a ringing vote of confidence for 1955 from the directors. He also got some coaching help for the '55 season, assistants Clem Crowe and Vic Lindskog, and switched to the T-formation. The best of his new players were quarterback Arnie Galiffa, a superb passer from Army, versatile backfielder Primo Villanueva and receiver Danny Edwards.

Things got better in 1955 (that year the slogan was "The Lions Will Thrive in '55") but not much and, apparently, not enough. The Lions won five games that season, including both ends of a Labour Day weekend double-header on the prairies. The team flew home from that one, landed at 3:00 a.m. and were greeted by 1,000 fans and a brass band. But the music died and a five-game win season wasn't enough. Stukus, the only Canadian coach in the Canadian Football League, was fired.

Immediately after the last game, he was called before a directors' meeting. There was a general discussion on the team's progress, with all the directors speaking. Stukus was asked to leave the meeting, and when he was called back in the three-person executive committee told him he was through as coach. There was a vague suggestion of another job with the team. The vote was 13-10. Five members of the board were absent, and president Don Mackenzie, who had replaced Art Mercer, did not vote.

Mackenzie said at the time, "I feel lower than I have ever felt in my life. I hope I never have to go through anything like this again." He added, "I feel there were no internal politics involved and would be very disappointed if there were."

Bill Clancey still disputes that statement. One of the few still-living founding directors, Clancey maintains, "Stuke was double-crossed. I voted to keep him on. All the long-time directors voted for him, but the Johnny-come-latelys voted to fire him. We would never have had a football team without Stuke. He started with nothing and he broke his ass for the team. He went all over the province selling the team and, in the end, a few directors sold him out."

The firing set the entire city ablaze. One club member, Phil Wood, invoked Section 19 of the club's bylaws, which said the directors must call an extraordinary meeting on the written demand of a hundred members. Wood got enough signatures on a petition and a meeting was called. There were demands that Stukus be rehired and the directors fired. But Stukus wasn't buying it. He told the meeting, in effect, thanks but no thanks; he was tired of working for too many bosses.

He still remembers his feelings. "They offered me a job as assistant to the president, an office boy job, and I didn't want it. There had always been a core of half a dozen directors who were looking to buy the club for themselves. All they wanted to do was keep operating costs down to keep the price of the team down. They cost me a lot of players. When I went to that protest meeting they told me they were going to fire the bosses and turn the team over to me. I just told them, forget it. I had had it. The whole thing had become a bit sordid."

Stukus's assistant, Clem Crowe, who had won a Grey Cup as the Ottawa Rough Rider coach in 1951, was made head coach of the Lions. Stukus became football editor of the Vancouver *Sun* at a salary far higher than he had ever made in football. He took the new job seriously.

"I watched Crowe's moves. He cut Arnie Weinmeister. He cut Arnie Galiffa and kept Tony Teresa, who was so short he couldn't see over the line of scrimmage. I figured the directors who wanted to buy the team were pulling his strings so I told him, 'Clem, I may have to get rid of you.' He said, 'But Stuke, I've got ten kids.'"

Herb Capozzi, a Kelowna-born Rhodes scholar who had played

tackle with Calgary and Montreal, was brought in as Lions general manager at the start of the 1957 season. Capozzi brought great marketing skills to the team, but that wasn't reflected on the field. Crowe's teams won only ten games in the next two seasons. Three straight losses into the 1958 season, Crowe left the stadium to find all four tires on his car had been slashed. The unkindest cut came the next day: he was sacked. Former end Dan Edwards was brought back from his three-hundred-acre Texas goat ranch to finish up the season, three wins and another seven losses. One journalistic wit suggested Edwards was cursed: he had three hundred goats in Waco and twenty-eight more in Vancouver. When Edwards applied for a contract extension for 1959, he had already arranged to bring in an assistant coach from Baltimore. The directors were not impressed—they had never heard of a fellow named Don Shula—and Edwards, too, went down the road.

Instead, Wayne Robinson, Bud Grant's defensive coach, was brought in from Winnipeg on a one-year contract, and he imported Dave Skrien, a one-time Bomber player, as his backfield coach. Robinson signed three players from the University of Iowa Rose Bowl team, Randy Duncan and running backs Willie Fleming and Bob Jeter.

Duncan's passing and Fleming's brilliant running produced a 9-7 season and a spot in the western semi-finals, where they were outscored 61-15 by Edmonton. But the B.C. team had made the playoffs for the first time. Attendance hit 243,604, and there was euphoria in Vancouver. It would last only until 1960, when the team fell to 5-9-2 and missed the playoffs.

At the end of the 1959 season, Robinson had been given a new four-year contract, with unprecedented power clauses, and that began to grate on the team's critics, the membership and the media. It was suggested that the directors had made a dangerous blunder in giving out a four-year contract, that Robinson had too much control. It was suggested that he had his lunch eaten by Calgary in the 1961 trade that brought in quarterback Joe Kapp in exchange for Jim Walden, Bruce Claridge, Bill Crawford and Ed Obradovich. Kapp, a Rose Bowl star, had worn out his welcome in Calgary after two seasons, and everybody knew his knees were shot, right? Why gamble that much on a lame horse? And, true to Stukus's dire prediction in 1955, two groups of directors put forward offers to buy the club. They were both shouted down at a rancorous meeting of two thousand of the $20 card-holders.

Six losses and a tie into the 1961 season, Robinson was fired. In a six-line, fifty-five-word press release, team vice-president Alan Eyre announced that Skrien would replace Robinson for the rest of the season and that the team would eat the remaining years on Robinson's contract. The decision was made by twenty-three directors in a secret ballot, twenty days after they had given Robinson a vote of confidence. The ballots were destroyed.

Skrien said at the time, "I always wanted to be a head coach, but I never wanted to get a job this way." Under him, the team won one game and tied one over the rest of a dreadful season.

But while Skrien, a gum-chewing perfectionist, may have accepted with reluctance, he was inheriting an emerging team. In addition, the entire structure of the B.C. Lions operation had been forced into reform by a barber named Sam. Sam Salloum was an original 1953 card-carrying member who was about to become as great a hero as any player. Salloum walked the streets of Vancouver between haircuts collecting names on a petition to have the entire operation of the team put under review. Some dismissed him as a crank, but he got enough signatures to force a meeting and, as a paper compromise, the directors agreed to call in outside consultants. The result was the landmark McPherson Report. Don McPherson, a former WIFU president, Edmonton past president Al Anderson and Calgary Stampeders backer and wealthy industrialist Frank McMahon conducted meetings in Vancouver with directors, players and sportswriters. Their conclusions were damning: they said the directorate was top-heavy, the constitution unworkable and the executive without direction. They recommended that ten directors be cut, with power placed in the hands of a small executive committee, and that the responsibilities of the coach and the general manager be more clearly defined. Out of that emerged a more efficient operation under the direction of a visionary new president, C. B. "Slim" Delbridge.

One of the new directors who came in under Delbridge was a young Vancouver lawyer and former rugby star named Al McEachern. McEachern still considers the McPherson Report a pivot point for the

Lions. "The investigation, the report and the reforms were absolutely necessary. Since 1954 we had been in the playoffs once. Annual meetings were like zoos. The team was being run like a country club and directors were being elected in popularity contests. There were factions trying to buy the team in spite of the membership's wish to keep it public. Something had to be done. We needed a new broom. Delbridge brought real business sense to the operation. He brought in some new directors and brought back some of the old ones. And for a while we had great short-term success. But four years later we slipped back to the same situation we had before the McPherson Report." McEachern's analysis carries the weight of judicial wisdom. He went on to become Lions president, WIFU president, commissioner of the CFL, chief justice of the Supreme Court of B.C. and chief justice of the Appeal Court of B.C.

In the new state of grace, Skrien built a winner. Team physician Dr. Hec Gillespie rebuilt the wreckage of Kapp's knees, and trainer Roy Cavallin performed taping miracles to keep the team leader mobile enough to pile up passing yardage with receivers Fleming, Pat Claridge and Sonny Homer. Fleming became the most exciting running back in the country, augmented by fullback Nub Beamer, a slashing short-yardage runner and a devastating pass-blocker. Defensive coach Jim Champion developed the Headhunters, a big, mobile defensive team anchored at middle linebacker by Tom Brown, ends Dick Fouts and Mike Martin, hometown tackle Mike Cacic, the great veteran corner linebacker Norm Fieldgate and Canadian safety Neal Beaumont.

The Lions went 12-4 in 1963, their first-ever first-place finish, beat Calgary in the playoffs and hosted Hamilton in the Grey Cup game. The team was just as successful at the box office. Season tickets sales were up to 18,000. They drew 251,712, including a Canadian record of 35,704 for a game against Calgary, and welcomed their one-millionth fan on October 19. The club had $200,000 in the bank.

But a harsh reality check was delivered by the Tiger-Cats in the Grey Cup game. They beat the injury-wracked Lions 21-10, and Angelo Mosca, with a marginally late hit that knocked Fleming out of the game, earned the lasting hatred of Vancouver. The wound never healed because Mosca kept picking it. In his post-season career in professional wrestling,

Mosca revived his villain image every time he came to Vancouver, saying things like, "It was a good, clean hit . . . Fleming quit, that's all." He later told sports columnist Archie McDonald that the controversy "made my career. It made me a national figure. I got some commercials, got to speak at banquets and when I started wrestling, it automatically made me the bad guy. I was smart enough to market myself. There were a million stories written about me and they all helped."

The Lions loss was a crushing disappointment to Vancouver fans—the Vancouver *Sun* put out a post-game Extra with the huge headline "Aw Nuts!"—but was no surprise to the phlegmatic Skrien. He wrote in *Countdown to Grey Cup*, the book on the 1963-64 seasons he co-wrote with the late Dick Beddoes, that he knew the night before the game his team was not ready: "There was a feeling—probably it got to me too late—that it wasn't quite so important to win the Grey Cup as to play in it. Lethargy in a team is the toughest rust for a coach to knock off. I honestly didn't feel in my heart that we were going to win because of the feeling of the squad . . . I knew the B.C. Lions were in trouble for our first crack at the national championship. Starry eyes weren't going to stare down tomorrow's enemy. The Hamilton Tiger-Cats are hardy philosophers who believe in winning if they have to cut ears and gouge eyes to do it."

But Skrien kept faith. He had the 1963 Grey Cup champagne put away under lock and key. Before the 1964 season began he had a new house built, and at the corner of the fireplace he had a niche put in, to the dimensions of the Grey Cup.

His faith was rewarded. The Lions dominated the West again with an 11-2-3 record that put six players (including the retreaded Kapp) on the CFL all-star team. Skrien was coach of the year, and his team went to Toronto for a rematch with the Tiger-Cats. There were no starry eyes this time, just suppressed determination from a great football team. They beat Hamilton 34-24, even scoring a touchdown on a fumbled field goal snap, holder Pete Ohler alertly passing to Jim Carphin on an emergency play they had often discussed.

The Lions cracked that mellow champagne and flew home—almost without the Grey Cup. It had been left in their hotel and was recovered just minutes before flight time west. Massive crowds, ankle-deep in rainwater, greeted the team back at the Vancouver airport. Skrien voiced a few platitudes, then drove home and put the Grey Cup up on his fireplace. It had taken eleven years, $7 million, a couple of revolutions, five coaches and 757 players of all ranks, but the B.C. Lions had finally grown to adulthood.

Those two grand seasons proved to the country that the B.C. Lions could, indeed, do something right. But the following year proved they couldn't do it right for very long. The decline of the new empire was as quick as the climb up had been slow. Shockingly, the defending champions fell to a 6-9-1 record in 1965 and a fourth-place finish.

Coroners are still performing autopsies on the 1965 team. There were injuries, but it is widely believed that the team got fat in the head, that the defensive and offensive teams split away from each other, that Kapp was an agitator who had lost respect for Skrien. Some players had drawn on their contracts to plunge on a stock touted by a former player. Some of them were wiped out and played the season without pay cheques. The most bizarre theory is that a province-wide brewery strike in B.C. deprived the club of the post-practice beer busts that had brought them together in 1964. (After one road trip in Regina, Champion bought all the beer the equipment truck could carry. When airport personnel told him the flight was overloaded, Champion ordered the beer aboard and arranged for the equipment to come on a later flight.)

But whatever the root cause, Vancouver football fans were to be revisited by all their worst demons. Nineteen sixty-six was the year of the two Joe Kapp affairs.

The Vancouver Sun put out

a post-game Extra with the

headline "Aw Nuts!"

Firstly, Kapp cost Lions offensive coach Frank "Blacky" Johnston his job. On an eastern trip in September, Johnston caught Kapp coming into the team hotel four hours after team curfew. Johnston went to Skrien and said that Kapp had to be disciplined for the good of the team, sent home or benched in favour of backup Pokey Allen. Skrien declined. There was an argument. After the team returned to Vancouver, Skrien announced that Johnston had resigned for reasons of ill health.

Vancouver football writers were skeptical. Jim Taylor wrote, "If Johnston was sick, it was with nausea. He wasn't ready to quit; he was ready to fight. And what he was fighting was the system he felt was protecting the little group of non-producing prima donnas who have greased the skids for the Lions." Jim Kearney wrote in his column, "Here is a football team that has been largely destroyed by a yahoo player clique whose playboy antics and undermining of the coach have split the team in two. [But] instead of the quarterback being sent home and suspended until his over-inflated ego simmered down to something approaching normalcy, an assistant coach was offered up as a sacrifice."

The sacrifice just borrowed a bit of time for Skrien. After a worse year of 5-11 in 1966, he was fired in the middle of the 1967 season, with Jim Champion returning from the St. Louis Cardinals to finish off a 3-12-1 season. And by the summer of '67, Kapp was gone, too, suspended for signing a contract with the Houston Oilers while still under contract to B.C. Claim and counterclaim wound through several court levels. But Kapp was finished in Vancouver, after having run for 20 touchdowns and passed for 97 in five seasons.

Chief Justice McEachern remembers, "Joe was worried he would have to sit out a year. He kept coming to me and asking for advice. I kept saying, 'I can't even talk to you. You're suing us.' Joe begged me to make a deal where he could play in a warm climate, California or Florida. He didn't want to go to a cold place like Minnesota or Green Bay. But the only offer we got for him was $50,000 from the Vikings so that's where he went, as a backup to Gary Cuozzo. In two years, he took them to the Super Bowl."

Herb Capozzi left the team to enter politics. Willie Fleming, Tom Hinton and Tom Brown retired because of accumulated injuries. Fleming left behind enviable records: 37 touchdowns rushing, 48 receiving, and a career average of 7.1 yards per rush. The Lions traded his NFL rights to Minnesota for Canadian receiver Jim Young, who became the team's greatest career receiver. Champion lasted a season and a half before he was replaced by Jackie Parker, and then the rock-steady Eagle Keys. And so the first two decades of B.C. Lions football ended, too few roars, much too many catcalls.

There would be more of the same in the decades to come: four more trips to the Grey Cup, two of them victorious; seven more head coaches (not including Jim Young's one-game term); the problematic turn to private ownership; the move into the domed B.C. Place Stadium; a decline in attendance; bankruptcy; revival.

But the 1950s and 1960s had been a roller-coaster ride, and no one spent more time in the front car than Norm Fieldgate and Bob Ackles. One of the originals, corner linebacker Fieldgate played 223 games between 1954 and 1967, then became a director, and is still president of the Lions Alumni Club. "For a young guy coming out of junior football in Saskatoon, it was just a great experience. That first season, we started with the single wing, but after about fifteen backfield fumbles, we moved the quarterback under centre. Those days, fans cheered when we got a first down. They didn't expect much, we didn't give them much. Over the years, there was great camaraderie. It was a treat to be a defensive player on the sideline to watch Fleming run. When Kapp needed a first down, he'd grind it out himself. We had great, tough players, like Niemi and Weinmeister, Urban Henry, Tom Hinton, Ken Sugarman, Mike Cacic.

"It seemed in my last three years everything went against us, a lot of turmoil, tempers got short. But overall I loved it, great training camps, great times, great laughs."

Bob Ackles spent thirty-four and a half years with the Lions, going from water boy to general manager. Currently he is director of football operations with the Miami Dolphins, after previous shifts with the Dallas Cowboys and the Phoenix Cardinals. But he has never forgotten his Vancouver days. "We had just moved from Ontario when Vancouver got the franchise in 1953. I was fifteen when I applied for the water boy's job. I went to the first tryout camp and Stuke turned me over to the equipment manager, Tiger Kozak."

Ackles left his bucket and dipper and moved up the chain of command: assistant equipment manager, equipment manager, minor football co-ordinator, assistant general manager, then general manager in 1975. Mostly it was a labour of love.

"I never made a career decision at the start, but every time I got moved up, I wanted to move up higher. In 1953 the job cost me car fare. In

1954 they paid me $100. I was going to high school and selling sporting goods on the side and one year when my parents moved out of town, I slept in the equipment room. I got $500 from the club in 1960, the year Kay and I got married. I didn't start drawing a regular pay cheque until 1961, when Robinson fired the equipment manager and put me in the job. Until I left Vancouver in the summer of 1986 to go to Dallas, it had all been just pure excitement."

Any regrets? "Sure. I had two 1-15 seasons, the first year in Vancouver and Jimmy Johnston's first year in Dallas. Two years like those are enough for any career."

Why was there so little sustained success in Vancouver? Perhaps former premier W.A.C. Bennett answered that in 1966 when Herb Capozzi was sworn into the B.C. legislature as a rookie Social Credit backbencher. A beaming Capozzi said, "It's great to be on your team, sir. A team is only as strong as its weakest link, and we've got a great team."

The pragmatic Bennett growled, "That may apply to teams and it may apply to chains but it does not apply to political parties or governments. A government is not as strong as its weakest link, it's only as strong as its most brilliant mind."

Maybe the Lions had been doing it wrong all those years.

CHAPTER EIGHT

Local Heroes:
Saskatchewan Roughriders

A bleak night in Regina, September 1963. The air temperature and the mood of 20,000 spectators at Taylor Field were the same: bitter cold and dropping.

The Roughriders football team had been on a losing streak that looked fit to be extended. They were playing the despised Edmonton Eskimos, and they had had a terrible first half, reasonably competent on defence but unable to generate any wattage of offensive power under the direction of their new quarterback. The new guy was a baby-faced runt, and a marked-down bargain of a runt to boot. Ron Lancaster had spent the previous two seasons with the Ottawa Rough Riders, competing with Russ Jackson for the starting job in a running controversy that rivalled anything that steamed off Parliament Hill. In his rookie season with

Ottawa, Lancaster even played defence, tackling powerfully and intercepting three passes in one game. Lancaster had started the 1960 Grey Cup game but was quickly replaced by Jackson, who took Ottawa to victory as Lancaster watched from the bench. The Ottawa coach, Frank Clair, realized he had gold in Jackson: a player good enough to start and a Canadian who did not count against his import ratio. Lancaster was expendable.

Ottawa sent Lancaster west for $500, but with an interesting proviso in the deal: if Saskatchewan ever decided to cut him, Ottawa would have the first right of refusal on reacquiring him. They didn't want Lancaster returning to another eastern team with thoughts of revenge rattling around in his crew-cut cranium. Lancaster's initial wish was to go to Montreal, but the western Riders assured him that he would get every opportunity to be a starter. He made the move, bought a house and got a teaching job. And he got a whole new life.

Now, on this chilly September, it appeared that half the $500 purchase price must have been for good will, and the purchase of a house rashly optimistic. The chilled and disenchanted fans, with grand memories of previous quarterbacks Glenn Dobbs and Frank Tripucka the only thing warming them, were unloading their displeasure on the five-foot, nine-inch Lancaster and his mercurial coach, Bob Shaw.

Saskatchewan football fans had discovered in his two seasons that Shaw, a magnificent receiver in his playing days in the United States and Canada, had a volcanic temper attached to a dangerously short fuse. He would often streak down the sidelines, clipboard flying, in pursuit of a referee, eventually running out from under his headset, which would hover in the air for a few seconds like a cartoon character's hat. His blazing haranguing of his own players could be heard in the highest seats.

But when, the crowd wondered, would Shaw deal with his malfunctioning, undersized quarterback?

Lancaster came off the field, head down. Shaw met him. To the surprise of the spectators, the tall coach wrapped his arm around the little quarterback's shoulder and leaned close to speak to him, like a fond father, it seemed, whispering forgiveness.

Actually, Shaw was hissing, "That's about it for you. One more

interception and you're back in Springfield, Ohio, in time for supper—
tomorrow."

Shaw sat Lancaster down and sent the thirty-five-year-old, arm-
weary Tripucka in to run the offence. Tripucka threw three interceptions.
Shaw was near flashpoint and meltdown. With the game running down
and a nothing-left-to-lose sense of doom, Shaw sent Lancaster back in to
finish out a lost cause. It was hardly an act of kindness. There were seven
minutes left on the clock. The Riders had the ball on their own 1-yard
line facing into a stiff wind. They huddled up deep in their own end zone.
Lancaster set out to salvage the game and his football life.

Handing the ball off to his fullback, and throwing short passes to a
rookie end, he moved them down the field. Twice he ran the ball himself
on third down and made it. From Edmonton's 8, he faked inside to his
fullback, stuck the ball on his hip and scuttled into the end zone. He had
used up six of the seven remaining minutes to take his team 109 yards to
score the winning touchdown in an 8-7 victory.

That performance saved Lancaster's job. It did not convince Shaw,
but the chilled crowd went home warm and intrigued. Maybe this kid
did have something going for him. It was, of course, impossible at that
time to divine just what a telling moment that fraction of a ball game in
1963 would be. Bob Shaw would leave at the end of the following season,
to know only in retrospect what he had unwittingly created and left
behind. He would become a footnote; Ron Lancaster would become a
legend.

The $500 quarterback from Wittenberg College (which also gave the
world Isaac Funk and Adam Wagnalls, the dictionary boffins) would play
288 games for the Riders over the next sixteen years. They would win 170
of them, and he would lead them to the playoffs fourteen times.
Lancaster, who became known as the Little General, would win two
Schenley Awards as the outstanding player in Canada. He would play
fifteen straight seasons without missing a game. He was the all-Canadian
quarterback four times, and Western all-Star seven times. He is in both
the Canadian Football and the Canadian Sports halls of fame. He would
play until he was forty-one, for nineteen years in the CFL, and it would be
his proudest boast that he was never carried off the field. He always said

that his worst nightmare was the spectre of being flattened on the field, some hooting enemy lineman standing over him waving a triumphant fist. They don't keep statistics on pain bitten back, but Lancaster played tough and he played hurt, and Taylor Field fans loved him for it. It would be a long, long time before Ron Lancaster would be booed in Taylor Field again.

And there was more. The straight-ahead, smash-face runner Lancaster employed on that 109-yard march, rookie fullback George Reed, would become the greatest ground-gainer in the team's history. And the useful receiver, playing his first game that historic night, that was Hugh Campbell. He, too, would pile up magical yardage, turning the eccentrically shaped Taylor Field end zones into his own artistic gallery. From a game that began so bleakly emerged a dynastic football team that created a unique, feverish condition called Rider Pride.

Football in Regina has survived everything that God and Mother Nature could throw at it.

The heart of Saskatchewan football pumps thunderously in Regina. Like the human heart, it receives life-sustaining blood from the veins, then pumps it through the arteries of the province. The blood receives a fresh supply of oxygen in the lungs; the lungs of Taylor Field football fans are the strongest in this country. The precious bodily fluid is circulated and recirculated through the network of highways, secondary roads and dirt roads that crisscross the province.

Saskatchewan today is a province of fewer than a million hardy people scattered across 651,900 square kilometres of hard geography. Regina is a city of 180,000. Taylor field seats 27,732. These are not healthy figures for a major league sports franchise. But Roughrider football survives on community ownership and province-wide support. Saskatchewan has 200,000 kilometres of roads—cross-province, city and rural—and all of them lead to Taylor Field. When current general manager Al Ford is told that the big-city view of Roughrider football is that of a family in Weyburn loading up the pickup truck and driving through a blizzard to get to the game, he differs only slightly: "Yes, a blizzard of snow in the winter, a blizzard of mosquitoes in the summer." (When Taylor Field seating was increased temporarily in advance of the 1995 Grey Cup game, and every new seat was sold for a league game, the stadium was the third-largest "city" in the province.)

Football has been around and feverish in Regina since 1910. It has survived everything that God, Mother Nature and Saskatchewan's own harsh climate could throw at it. The city and the province survived the terrible summer cyclone of 1912 that killed twenty-eight people, injured two hundred and destroyed five hundred buildings, including Dominion Park, the Roughriders' first home, which was blown flat.

Football survived when the team treasury contained exactly thirty cents going into the season. In the early years, the team used one football for the entire game and then raffled it off, at twenty-five cents a pop. Football survived seasons when the team was so short of funds and equipment that players coming off the field had to strip off their sweaters and hand them to players who were going onto the field. It survived six years of disastrous Dust Bowl droughts in the thirties, when the team and its supporters kept faith in the only way they could: many farmers traded bushels of their own diminished wheat crops for season tickets. To this day, the unofficial slogan of Rider football is that coined by a former player, coach and team manager, the legendary Al Ritchie, who used to hook his thumbs in his vest and advise, "Buy May wheat and bet on the Roughriders." It's as valid today as it was in the dry, unforgiving Depression years.

Football in Saskatchewan has never been a mere entertainment option as it is in bigger provinces; it is a moral precept. The Regina *Leader-Post*'s editorial page once thundered, "It is not an act of charity to subscribe to the ticket fund, but the performance of a civic duty. Even though one never sees a game, a contribution should be made."

Another time, a Regina sportswriter wrote, "Folks here got to talking football during the last week. The gossip spread beyond the ordinary sporting circle. It flowed back into the bays and inlets of Saskatchewan pride and Regina prestige. A delegation of Saskatoon citizens of good repute landed in Regina Saturday morning to see the game. A big Moose

Jaw contingent came out of the west and bought up the price of admission. Weyburn and Yorkton rushed in their delegations.

"Far out in the prairies, old grads of western universities, former players, two-chin men who once played in their lithesome youth heard the roar of the crowd on far playing fields, caught the fever and headed for Regina. When the battle was ready to begin, nearly 5,000 people were on hand. At a dollar a head and fifty cents for the youngsters who stood for the game, the gate ran into the price of a couple of improved farms, which isn't such a bad showing for a depressed territory."

Annis Stukus, who took Edmonton Eskimo and B.C. Lions teams into Taylor Field, says that the ferocious partisanship of Roughrider fans was a force to be reckoned with. "It could get scary in there, believe me. Before they put in the extra seats, they had so many people standing all around the sidelines, eight and ten yards deep, that a running back would be worried about going out of bounds and never coming back. I used to worry when I went to the field to kick a field goal, wearing my wrist watch, that they'd come after my helmet and my watch. The fans were raucous, vocal, downright intimidating, and part and parcel of the Green Machine."

The success of any professional sports franchise can be found down at the bottom line of its season ticket subscribers, the individuals who pledge their money now for expected entertainment to come. But the Riders have a more tangible article of faith. It is a sturdy brass plaque on a wall of its offices, both a gazetteer of the province and a marriage certificate. On the plaque, which was dedicated at the team's silver anniversary in 1977, are the names of 304 cities, towns, villages, hamlets and rural communities that have pledged their support to the football team. It is a roll of honour that pleases the ear: Assiniboia, Biggar, Cudworth, Cut Knife, Kipling, Porcupine Plain, Moosomin, Saltcoats, Goodsoil, Oxbow, Wawata, Uranium City, Antler, Drinkwater, Eyebrow, Elbow, Holdfast, Killaly, Plenty, Turtleford, Tuxford and Zenon Park.

The people from these geographic dots do more than sit around in their coffee shops talking Roughriders. They support the Riders with their dollars, their vehicles and their feet. Toronto writer Trent Frayne, raised on big-city football, loves to tell the story of a travelling salesman who got caught up in Rider Pride and thought he was part of a *Twilight Zone* script. The man decided to get a jump on the next week's work by visiting some of his small-town clients on a Saturday. He drove into Fillmore and found every store in town locked and shuttered. Same thing in Creelman; not even a coffee shop was open. Fearing some kind of holocaust had occurred while he was on the road, he found a phone booth and called ahead to some clients in Arcola and Stoughton. The phones rang and rang, but no one answered. Finally, seeing a small boy on a bicycle, he asked where everyone was. The boy gave him a look of juvenile contempt and said, "At home with the radio, or in Regina for the football game."

This community involvement, widespread yet close, had positive benefits. Eagle Keys, who played in Montreal and Edmonton and coached in Edmonton, Regina and Vancouver, says that football in Regina was community policed. "There was no place for a player to hide in Regina. If he was out drinking, we'd get a call from a citizen the next morning. Guys tended to behave themselves or do their partying in their own homes with their teammates and families, which was great for team spirit. In Vancouver there were too many places and we couldn't keep up with our players."

For players coming to Saskatchewan on trades from bigger places, or recruited from major American universities, the smallness and the extreme heat and cold of the seasons could be daunting. One highly recruited import landed at the Regina airport, watched a prairie hailstorm rolling across the sky like a dirty carpet and took the same plane back home.

But Vancouver lawyer Jim Carphin recalls the charm of Regina when he was traded there after five seasons with the B.C. Lions. "I got off the plane, rented a car and drove out to find Ron Atchison's place. I found the block and knocked at a door. A guy came out and said, 'Atch's place? End of the block. You can't miss it. It's the house with the chickens on the roof.'

"In Vancouver, we had a training table every night after practice, all you could eat: roasts, steaks, three or four vegetables, salads, desserts. When we came in from practices in Regina, freezing cold, the trainer,

Sandy Archer, would serve us his homemade soups and garlic sausage on crackers.

"I got a serious eye injury there. I was in hospital with both my eyes bandaged. The doctors wouldn't let me leave because I had no relatives in town to take care of me. One of the broadcasters mentioned this on the radio, and the same day a lady came and took me home. She, her husband and their kids took care of me around the clock. I'll never forget that kindness."

The love affair with the Riders had to put up with some accommodation and some radical changes. Up until 1924, the team was known as the Regina Rugby Football Club. The name "Roughriders" was adopted at a time when the Ottawa Rough Riders had temporarily changed their name to the Ottawa Senators. But that Roughrider name was not entirely new in 1924. It had been hanging around informally since 1890, applied to members of the North-West Mounted Police who broke the force's horses and affixed to a police rugby football team by the *Free Press* during a team visit to Winnipeg. It was not until 1948 that the Regina Roughriders became the Saskatchewan Roughriders, the name enlarged to the satisfaction of everyone in the province. Annis Stukus admits that it was this wise move that prompted him in 1954, when he came out west to coach the new Vancouver team, to urge the Lions directors to adopt a provincial name for their team. "I always remembered the time Normie Kwong and I were invited to speak at a Roughriders' fundraising dinner. There were seven hundred people there. We were told that five hundred of them came from outside Regina. That's when I realized the truth of Roughrider football: Regina wasn't big enough to support a franchise, but Saskatchewan was."

For the first thirty-six years of the team's existence, Roughrider fans rooted for the sacred red and black, the original team colours. The widely accepted reason for the colour change was purely economic. A Roughrider director, in Chicago on business, walked past a sporting goods store that was going out of business and selling its stock at distress prices. He couldn't resist the bargain of two complete sets of green and white football uniforms.

By 1950, the Roughriders had accepted a growing trend and were recruiting for two-platoon football. The club's executive, under president Robert Kramer, had been restructured to provide even more community involvement, and Kramer was lobbying the Western Interprovincial Football Union for a gate equalization plan. It was a time of profound change, and the most significant change of all was announced in the off-season. The Riders had lured Glenn Dobbs.

Born in Texas, raised in Oklahoma, a star at the University of Tulsa and with the Brooklyn Dodgers and the Los Angeles Dons of the U.S. professional leagues, Dobbs had been out of football for the 1950 season. At six feet, four inches, 210 pounds, he was a tall, charming, triple-threat player.

Roughrider fans met him for the first time at Regina's Grand Theatre on a brutal, −30° night. Every seat in the theatre was filled, and an equal number of people huddled outside. It was announced that Dobbs had turned down a two-year contract, at $17,500 a year, to play in Regina for two years at $12,500. The crowd loved him immediately when he explained that Regina was his kind of town. He said that to the crowd inside, and then went outside to say the same to the freezing folks on the sidewalk. He said later, "I hadn't seen such enthusiasm since my college days. Football really is a game of fun and friendship, and if you don't get that out of it, there's no sense in being in it. That's why I quit the American pros. It was the major reason I decided on Regina."

Dobbs became more than a player; he became a phenomenon, a social force. People put stickers on their car licences, proclaiming "Dobberville." It is said that when Saskatchewan kiddies balked at eating their peas or were sassy, their mothers would threaten to tell the Dobber. When Regina city council refused to finance the painting of Taylor Field's drab, two-block-long fences, farmers donated barn paint and forty volunteers, young and old, including Dobbs, got the job done in one day. Dobbs loved the remarkable career contrast. He said, "One year I'm all-pro in Los Angeles; the next I'm painting a fence in Regina."

But Dobbs was not the only prized pelt taken from the Riders' scouting trapline, just the glossiest. The team also brought in tackle Martin Ruby from the New York Yankees and Donald "Red" Ettinger, a place-kicking centre, from the New York Giants. The Riders talked running back Bob Sandberg out of retirement. Running backs Ken Carpenter and Bobby Marlow churned out tough yardage and took turns on defence. It was Marlow who ended the brief pro career of B.C. Lions running back Al Pollard with a crunching tackle that still reverberates around Vancouver's east end.

The new mix did not gel immediately. Dobbs lost sixteen pounds that first season, most of it shed while he was running for his life behind an inexperienced offensive line. But the Dobber was just as skilled on the field as he was gracious off the field. In the 1951 season, his first in Canada, he threw 28 touchdown passes and punted for a 44-plus yard average to lead the league. In one late-season game his first year, he threw 4 touchdown passes in the span of twenty-three minutes. He was a determined runner and a shrewd play-caller, and his prodigious punting made up for a lot of his teammates' offensive shortcomings. The only thing he was not was durable, despite the image many fans had of him as immortal. Dobbs got hurt. He played hurt, but the minor and serious injuries piled up, and by the end of his first season he was wounded.

But when Dobbs ran in the winning touchdown in the third game of the western playoff final against Edmonton in 1951, fans tore down the goalposts, paraded them downtown and around city hall and then planted them in the front yard of Dobbs's house on Montaigne Street. Dobbs took the Riders to the 1951 Grey Cup game, against Ottawa in Toronto, but he was in no condition to enjoy the experience. Going into the national final, he was admitting to a charley horse and keeping secret three broken ribs that required heavy padding. Dobbs was not the only Saskatchewan player on the hobble that day. Jack Russell, another tall Texan, who had scored 9 touchdowns and gained over 800 yards during the regular season, did not dress because of a knee injury. Among the walking wounded were Ettinger, who handled place-kicking chores while nursing bruised ribs, and stocky non-import Del "The Bulldog" Wardien, Saskatchewan's most dependable defensive halfback, who sprained an ankle in practice the week before the game. Two-way star backfielder Al Bodine also had a suspect ankle. Head coach Harry "Blackjack" Smith's options were curtailed, as by game time he was down to only twenty-eight players available for action.

Desperate for an edge, Smith had had trainer Sandy Archer bring along four types of shoes, appropriate for any playing conditions. There were long cleats for a muddy field, short cleats for a dry one, running shoes for a frozen field and, in case the turf at Varsity Stadium resembled the ice sheet at Maple Leaf Gardens, corrugated-rubber-soled lumber-jack boots of the type that the Eskimos had used against the Riders in the western final.

But from the opening whistle, Smith's team might as well have been wearing wooden clogs for all the good their footwear did them. For three quarters, the team from the nation's capital administered punishment to their prairie brethren, running up a 20-0 score. Then the pride of the western Riders came to the fore. Roy Wright, late of Regina's Scott Collegiate, pounced on a Benny MacDonnell fumble on the Ottawa 30. Two plays later, Dobbs hit tall import receiver Jack Nix for a touchdown. Ettinger fell on another Ottawa fumble. Dobbs sold a fake to the Ottawa defenders while ex-Regina junior star Sully Glasser plunged off tackle into the end zone. Two quick touchdowns on turnovers; one more and the game would be tied. But it was not to be. A last desperate pass attempt by Dobbs was picked off, and the gun sounded to end Saskatchewan's comeback.

Roughrider fans passed out fifteen thousand loaves of bread made with Saskatchewan wheat.

But what a trip it had been, ending nineteen years of frustration in Regina. Seven hundred fans had packed twenty-eight special train coaches to Toronto, where they passed out fifteen thousand loaves of bread made with Saskatchewan wheat. Twenty thousand of those who stayed home signed and sent a scroll of support. When the team returned home, they were cheered at a rally at which premier Tommy Douglas told the players that he had never had much luck impressing Ottawa either.

President Bob Kramer fired coach Smith minutes after the Grey Cup game for alleged misuse of personnel, and in 1952 Dobbs was made player-coach. In training camp, he suffered an injury that limited his ability to run and kick. The Riders lost Nix and Bodine to U.S. military service and veteran defensive end Jack Wedley to retirement. Many of the remaining players were in their late twenties or early thirties, their best years well behind them. The Riders went 3-13 that year, and the team began the arduous task of rebuilding, recruiting tough local kids like Harry Lampmann, Reg Whitehouse and Ron Atchison. Atchison, Whitehouse and Reg Clarke would anchor the Rider line for a total of forty seasons. Atchison played middle guard for sixteen years, eleven of them while wearing a cast on one arm with which he laid a world of pain on a lot of enemy centres. His legend was made permanent during a game played on an icy field. For traction, Atchison had wrapped a couple of turns of tape around his Hush Puppies street shoes. During a pile-up, an opposition player saw those brown shoes and cried out to the referee, "Unpile 'em! There's a civilian down there."

In 1953, Dobbs stepped aside as coach in favour of Frank Filchock, brought in from Edmonton, and the two of them alternated at quarterback in a season that fizzled out in a playoff series loss to Winnipeg. Bomber running back Lorne "Boom Boom" Benson ran for a record six touchdowns in one of those games.

In 1954, Canadian football expanded with the inaugural B.C. Lions but diminished by one star. Dobbs, still hobbled, was released and returned to coach in Tulsa. Dobberville went back to being Regina, the Riders went 10-4-2 but again lost to Winnipeg in the playoffs. Ron Lancaster was still a sixteen-year-old crew-cut kid in Fairchance, Pennsylvania, arguing with people who were telling him he was too small to play football. The years and the seasons rolled on.

Frank Tripucka passed for over 3,600 yards in 1956, but the Riders fell to Edmonton in the western playoffs. The Eskimos went east for the Grey Cup, but, as consolation, eight Roughriders went west for the Shrine All-Star Game in Vancouver two weeks later. The morning after the game, four Riders—Mel Becket, Mario DeMarco, Gordon Sturtridge and Ray Syrnyk, plus Sturtridge's wife, Mildred, and Winnipeg's massive middle guard, Calvin Jones—boarded Trans-Canada flight 810 to Regina. Somehow the aircraft smashed into Mount Slesse, a mist-shrouded slab of granite in B.C.'s Coast Range. All sixty-two passengers and the crew were killed. It was a week before the crash site was found by skilled mountain climbers, but because of the difficult terrain, the bodies were never recovered. The site was declared a shrine. The tragedy was underscored by the fact that Syrnyk and DeMarco had not been selected for the all-star game; they had gone to Vancouver to watch their Rider teammates play.

Not just the Roughrider team but the province of Saskatchewan was devastated by the deaths of the four popular young players. The Becket-DeMarco Trophy was established to recognize the outstanding lineman in the West, and the sweater numbers of the four players were retired.

Heart-wrenching death was not through with the Riders. It came back the following decade to take the life and spirit of Vernon Vaughan, a talented and dedicated end from Maryland State. The team's leading receiver in 1959, Vaughan was stricken with leukemia in 1961. He died three weeks after being diagnosed. In a poignant denouement, Vaughan, according to his wishes, was buried in his Roughriders sweater. The young man took his commitment to the green and white to the grave.

Understandably, perhaps, the Roughriders went into a five-year spiral after the Mount Slesse incident, winning only eighteen games from 1957 through 1961. George Terlep replaced Filchock as head coach and in turn was replaced by Tripucka, who was replaced by Ken Carpenter for one 2-14 season. That brought in the elderly Steve Owen, a reigning giant with the New York Giants for twenty-two years. Owen, working mostly from memory, raised the Riders from fourth in 1961 to third in 1962, when he was named CFL coach of the year. But Owen was good mostly for laughs in Regina.

The stories about Owen were legion. Once, in the second half of a home game, Owen heard the gun sound and turned to his players' bench, spat a gob of tobacco juice and said with drawling disgust, "Well, boys, there's another one you pissed away." An assistant coach diplomatically said to Owen, "Uh, coach, that's just the end of the third quarter." Another time, all through a game in Vancouver's Empire Stadium, Owen stood on the sideline under a west-coast deluge of icy rain, his light jacket and trousers becoming more and more sodden. One of his assistants appealed to the players, "Look at that. The old guy is risking pneumonia because he's tough and he loves the game. Can't you guys show some of that character?" The assistant was made a little wiser in the ways of psychology when, after the game, he watched Owen strip off the sopping jacket and pants, and then the second layer, a compete set of waterproofs that had kept him dry.

When Bob Shaw came in the following year, he lucked into the Owen legacy, a gelling defensive team that would go five straight games in 1963 without giving up a touchdown. But he also started the season with a quarterback he did not believe in, until Ron Lancaster *made* him believe. Former Regina sportswriter Laurie Artiss recalls, "Shaw used to make a big show of pulling a guy from the bench and sending him into the game with a play. But Ronnie told me the guy coming in usually would say, 'Coach says call something that will work.'"

Also starting his pro career in 1963 was a chunky running back from Washington State, George Reed. Some football observers say flat out that he was the greatest running back in the history of the Canadian game. He ran tough, he blocked, he caught passes and he faked brilliantly. Eagle Keys, who succeeded Shaw as coach, says, "A lot of guys piled up great yardage statistics. But there was never anyone as dependable on short yardage as George. When it was third and one, third and two, he'd always get you that tough yard or two." Certainly, Reed's career numbers bear out all the praise: 134 touchdowns, eleven seasons rushing more than 1,000 yards, six of them in a row.

Jim Carphin recalls how brilliantly Lancaster utilized the Reed threat. "We had the ball on someone's 3-yard line, third down. The obvious call was Reed, straight ahead, and that's what Ronnie called in the huddle. But as we broke he whispered to me, 'Run a curl.' He faked to Reed, pulled the ball back and lobbed it to me for the touchdown. There was no one near me. Everybody else was stacked up on George. It was important that even our guys thought Reed had the ball."

Hugh Campbell, a late cut from the San Francisco 49ers, joined the Roughriders in the middle of that same season and became a pass-catching phenomenon. He played only six seasons but he caught sixty touchdown passes and helped the Roughriders to three Grey Cup games. Nicknamed "Granny Grunt," he did not have an impressive physique or great speed, but he ran exact patterns and had dizzying moves. Additionally, he walked the Taylor Field end zones until he knew every inch of the grass and the fences. Two fine defensive backs, Garney

Henley of Hamilton and Craig Murray of B.C., suffered serious injuries when they crashed into those fences while trying to track Campbell in the Taylor Field end zone.

The Roughriders made the 1963 western semi-final something that will never be forgotten. Calgary Stampeders whipped the Riders 35-9 in the first game, held in Calgary, of the two-game, total-points series. The Rider defence was ineffective, Lancaster threw three critical interceptions, and the coroners in the media were tying a tag on the Rider toes. The second game was back in Taylor Field, the home club facing a 26-point deficit right from the kickoff. But Shaw, with nothing left to lose, made two moves. He activated Ed Buchanan, a halfback he had picked up from Calgary a few weeks earlier for $500—another $500 bargain—and put a sleeper play into the game. Why not? How much worse could things get?

On their second play, Lancaster threw the sleeper pass to Ray Purdin, slouching on the sideline right in front of the Calgary bench. It went for a 76-yard touchdown. Then Lancaster threw a scoring pass to Buchanan and another to Dick Cohee. Calgary kicked a couple of singles, but by the half their overall lead was down to 10 points. And, by that time, something typically Saskatchewanesque was happening. At the opening kickoff, there were 10,000 in the stands. But as word of the team's comeback filtered out over the radio, cars began jamming the roads to the stadium and another 6,000 people arrived for the second half, which saw more of the same. Buchanan and Cohee scored their second majors. Reed scored on the ground. The Rider defence stifled the Calgary attack. The Roughriders won the game 39-12, and the series by 1 point. Rider fans faithfully still recall that game as the Miracle of Taylor Field.

Miraculous as it was, it had taken everything out of the Roughriders, and they lost the western final to the B.C. Lions. But the bricks of a foundation had been laid. The good times were back.

The combative Shaw left to move east, and Eagle Keys was elevated to the job of head coach. From 1965 through 1970, the brilliant, witty Kentuckian amassed a 76-32 record and took the Riders into three Grey Cup games. His first order of business was to rebuild Lancaster's confidence. Now retired in Langley, B.C., Keys says, "Ronnie wasn't sure he wanted to stay in Regina or play any more football. I told him I needed him, that he was my starter. I built everything around him. I knew he had a great football mind, so I let him audible any time he wanted to. He didn't even have to call a play in the huddle, just come to the line, check the defence and call what he thought. He could always come up with something that would hurt the other guys."

In 1965, the Roughriders began one of the longest-running hexes in professional football. From September of 1965 to November of 1972, the Riders beat the B.C. Lions twenty-one straight times. Eagle Keys would eventually see both sides of that streak.

Everything came together for the Roughriders in 1966. They finished first in the West, beat Winnipeg in the final and, in a nice piece of irony, met Ottawa, the other Riders, in the Grey Cup game, played on the rain-soaked turf of Vancouver's Empire Stadium. Fifteen years had passed since Saskatchewan had been in the national final, and they came into this one 8-point underdogs to Ottawa, who had humbled the defending champion Hamilton Tiger-Cats 72-17 in the two-game, total-points eastern final.

It seemed the bookies had made a wise call when, with just 2:28 gone in the first quarter, Russ Jackson hit flanker Whit Tucker on a 61-yard pass and run for an Ottawa touchdown. But Saskatchewan defensive back Dale West picked off a Jackson pass and returned it to the Ottawa 9, Lancaster flipped a quick 6-pointer to all-star end Jim Worden, and the game was tied. Then Lancaster fired a sure interception to Ottawa defensive back Bob O'Billovich who, startled by Lancaster's generosity, tipped the ball to Saskatchewan halfback Allan Ford for another major. Jackson and Tucker connected again, this time on a broken play as the speedy flanker grabbed a pass at the Saskatchewan 37 and scampered untouched into the end zone, and the teams went into their locker rooms tied 14-14 at the half.

Somehow, Ottawa had held Saskatchewan's vaunted running attack to only 27 yards rushing. At halftime, Keys told Lancaster, "Take it to them with what we do best. Punch them with the running game." When the teams took the field for the second half, the best offensive line in the country—centre Ted Urness, guard Al Benecick and tackle Clyde Brock were voted all-Canada all-stars that year; guard Jack Abendschan was an all-star in the West—went to work. They ground their eastern opponents into bloody meat, as Reed and Buchanan added the balance of a game-total in rushing yardage. Hugh Campbell caught a ball that by all rights ought to have been a Lancaster completion to Ottawa defensive back Moe Racine in the Ottawa end zone to put Saskatchewan up by a touchdown. Then, at the 8:30 mark of the fourth quarter, George Reed blasted through a hole Abendschan had opened, up the middle from the Ottawa 31, trailing tacklers like burrs on a hound dog's tail, for another score. The Saskatchewan Roughriders won it, 29-14.

After fifty-four years and eight Grey Cup disappointments, Saskatchewan had one to hold and to own. It was very much a homebred victory for the local heroes. Ten players on that 1966 Grey Cup squad were products of junior football played against the backdrop of the tall prairie sky. Atch was the godfather, or more accurately, the grandfather, having been assumed directly from the Saskatoon Hilltops back in 1952. End Gord Barwell, linebacker brothers Wayne and Cliff Shaw and defensive back Ted Dushinski were also ex-Hilltoppers. On offence, the stiff spines of former Regina Rams ran straight up the middle, from centre Ted Urness to backup fullback Henry Dorsch; on defence was another Ram, halfback Larry Dumelie. Al Ford honed his versatile football skills at Regina Central High, Dale West at the University of Saskatchewan.

And there was another piece of irony. The losing quarterback, Russ Jackson, was named the player of the game, while the winning quarterback, Ron Lancaster, was the runner-up. Like the 1951 Roughriders and Tommy Douglas, Lancaster could not get a break out of Ottawa.

The Riders went into the next year's Grey Cup confident they could repeat. But all afternoon long, they were utterly buffaloed by the implacable, improvisational defence of the Hamilton Tiger-Cats. "We didn't know what the hell the Hamilton defence was doing out there," mumbled Eagle Keys after the game. "They just kept moving around and belting us." "They just lined up and ran right over us," chimed in assistant coach Jim Duncan. Normally mild-mannered halfback Ed Buchanan lost his cool, took a swing at Ti-Cat rookie Gord Christian and was ejected. Hamilton's big, agile linemen, particularly Angelo Mosca and

John Barrow, stunted around Saskatchewan's befuddled offensive line, while kamikaze defensive back Ted Page flung himself at Lancaster through the gaps, dropping him for losses of 11, 13 and 15 yards. For the sixth game in a row, the spirited Tiger-Cat defence denied its opponents a single touchdown, allowing the Riders only a single point in a 24-1 embarrassment.

Saskatchewan Roughriders went on to top the western standings three straight years to close out the decade, dropping the 1969 Grey Cup to Ottawa, and losing to Calgary in the playoffs in 1968 and 1970. Twice more under Lancaster, in 1972 and 1976, the Riders made the national final, but there would be no more Grey Cup victories for the Little Assassin of Taylor Field.

By the 1978 season, Ron Lancaster was facing his forty-first birthday and playing a backup role, which disgusted him. He played his last game at Taylor Field on October 22, playing the final ten minutes as the Riders blew a lead and lost to Winnipeg. Incredibly, the Taylor Field crowd booed Lancaster as he left the field. Perhaps those cold Saskatchewan winters shorten the memory.

But he went out in style a week later in Edmonton. It was Jackie Parker Day. Again, Lancaster came into the game with ten minutes left, his team trailing by 6 points. He took them to 2 touchdowns, scoring the second himself after waving off the field goal team. The Edmonton crowd gave him a standing ovation. Lancaster could not hide his happiness after the game: "To have everything go right in the last ten minutes of your career, you couldn't ask for more than that." He retired the next day.

Regina sportswriter Bob Hughes wrote of Lancaster, "He was everything the Roughriders franchise became. He was too small to survive in a big man's game, they said, but he survived, he dominated. He helped it grow up."

The Roughriders immediately named Lancaster as head coach. His first day on the job, he realized what his most immediate problem was. The glorious fifties and sixties were over, and he was the first Roughrider coach in sixteen years who did not have Ron Lancaster at quarterback.

CHAPTER NINE

The Last of the Breed:
Ottawa Rough Riders

His perfect teeth—and there seemed to be about fifty-six of them—sparkled like polished bathroom tiles. His close-cut hair was always in place, even when he stepped from a locker room shower. His muscled body was as trim as a carving. He spoke slowly, thoughtfully, as if costing out each word. Russ Jackson gleamed in all respects. He radiated purpose and poise, control and efficiency, self-confidence and intellectual excellence.

His biographer, Eddie McCabe, said, "His career might be a blueprint for any Canadian boy."

His first football coach said, "If any father could design an ideal son, Russ would be it."

When he reported to his first professional training camp, he wore a suit, shirt and tie and had a clean hankie in his pocket. He took the streetcar. Other candidates, who drove up on Harleys and in old station wagons, wearing jeans, T-shirts and cowboy boots, didn't even recognize him as a player.

After he played the final game of his career, twelve years later, a famous picture depicted him brandishing the Grey Cup. The other famous person in the picture was the prime minister of Canada, Pierre Elliott Trudeau, wearing a rose in his hat. And what was that look in Trudeau's eye as he looked at Lancaster—envy?

In this depiction of a life purely and triumphantly lived, where does the garbage truck fit in?

Every man has his grail and his cross. For the young Russ Jackson, there was no confident plan to grow to manhood and win the Grey Cup. What there was was the fear of mediocrity, of being forced by failure to sit in the wrong seat on the garbage truck. It was the bleak symbol that motivated him to become a perfect knight who would have sat easily at King Arthur's right hand.

When he was in kindergarten in Hamilton, according to McCabe, Jackson and the other kids were asked by their teachers what they wanted to do when they grew up. Little Russell, his big pink ears sticking out like the open front doors of a hippie's Volkswagen, smiled and said he wanted to be a garbageman. It might have been the fascination of any little boy with big trucks that make huge banging noises. But Russell was serious, as he proved when he added, "But I don't want to lift all those cans. I want to drive the truck."

Curiously, it almost came true for a brief time. In 1953, by now a well-muscled teen-ager, Jackson worked for the Hamilton district roads department, mostly filling and patching potholes. For a week he was reassigned to the garbage squad. On his first run, Jackson was the swamper, jumping in and out of the passenger seat to pick up cans and hand them up to the guy who stood knee-deep in the grapefruit rinds and spaghetti tins, tamping the mess down with his boots. On the second run, the tamper told Jackson to switch with him. Jackson flatly refused, threatened to quit on the spot. The driver sided with Jackson.

That's the way it would always be. Russ Jackson would take trash from no one. The garbage truck did not haunt him, it motivated him. When it was second and long against the wind, when he was dealing contract hardball with team officials, he would dig in his cleats and set his standards. For the rest of his life, Jackson would be in the driver's seat.

The Privy Council didn't officially declare 1969 to be Russ Jackson Year. He did it himself, by inference and performance.

This is what Jackson's life looked like in 1969.

1. He was voted all-Canadian quarterback for the third time.
2. He was voted all-Eastern quarterback for the sixth time.
3. He won the Jeff Russell Trophy as the outstanding player in the East.
4. He won the Schenley Award as the outstanding CFL player for the third time.
5. He won the Schenley Award as the outstanding Canadian player for the fourth time.
6. Sports editors across the country voted him the outstanding athlete of the year.
7. News editors across Canada voted him the most newsworthy Canadian outside of public affairs.
8. He was awarded the Order of Canada.
9. He was honoured by Ottawa football fans with a Russ Jackson Day.
10. He was voted the most valuable player in the Grey Cup game, which Ottawa won.

Had there been time, Jackson might have extended the St. Lawrence Seaway to the Manitoba border and brought Quebec into the constitutional fold, but there are only so many hours in any man's day. And Jackson, recognizing a peak when he saw one, retired the day after the national final. He had done all there was.

Ottawa was established as Bytown in 1847, incorporated as the city of Ottawa in 1855 and made the capital of Canada in 1867. The Ottawa football club was formed in 1876 and established in 1898 as the Rough Riders, after the hardy loggers who rode rolling logs down the Ottawa River in the log drives. For reasons obscure—perhaps to borrow some glamour from the Stanley Cup–winning hockey team of the same name—they were renamed the Senators in 1924, but returned to the Rough Riders name two years later.

Through a century-plus of living side by side, Ottawa's two major institutions—Parliament and the Rough Riders—have shown consistent ability to dominate, to punish, to disappoint and to tax their supporters. Ottawa teams have won nine Grey Cups (Senators two, Rough Riders seven) and lost six. But right from the kickoff, they evidenced an early and abiding ability to raise hell, and to raise quirkiness to towering levels.

The first Grey Cup year was 1909, although the championship trophy was not completed and awarded for some months after the title game. As things turned out, Ottawa didn't get to the game, but they set a standard for enthusiasm that year for the hybrid game of fourteen-man rugby-football.

Ottawa management thought their 1909 team was so good that it insured sixteen players for $1,000 each; the policies would have returned $10 a week for life in the case of game-incurred disability. The coverage was prompted by a player the previous season who suffered knee injuries so severe he had to go to Scotland for surgery that cost him $200.

Thus protected, the 1909 team finished the season tied for first place with Hamilton, with 5-1 records. A playoff was dictated on neutral territory, Toronto. Interest in the game was so great that 2,300 tickets, released simultaneously in Ottawa, Hamilton and Toronto, sold out in two hours.

The Toronto *Globe* noted, "Five bands and the organized singing of the rooters' clubs from both football places made the football game look almost incidental to the demonstrations of their supporters.

"The Ottawa club came in early and no man who had red blood in his veins and could leave the Capital, stayed there Friday night. Hamilton chrysanthemums were everywhere about town by mid-day and altogether it was as big a football day as has been seen in Canada in many a year."

The Ottawa club, coached by Tom "King" Clancy, an Ottawa College student and later father of Francis "King" Clancy, the hockey figure of some repute, won the playoff 14-8 and assumed it was headed for the national final against the University of Toronto. But the trustees of the Grey Cup decided arbitrarily that they would honour a challenge from the Ontario Rugby Football Union. That meant that the Varsity-Ottawa game was downgraded to a semi-final.

Meanwhile, Clancy had an insurrection on his hands. His players claimed that team officials had bought up all the available tickets and there were none for their friends and relatives. The accused officials quickly made some tickets available. Whether the dispute was damaging is moot; what is known is that Varsity knocked Ottawa off with ease, 31-7, before a crowd of 12,000, and interest in the real championship game the following week fell off. Who cared about the little ORFU? Perhaps even Varsity made that dangerous assumption, because they had to rally with 20 second-half points to pull out a 26-6 victory over the Toronto Parkdale Canoe Club before only 3,907 spectators.

Three weeks after the 1909 season ended, Ottawa and Hamilton took their Canadian show on the road, accepting an invitation to play an exhibition game in New York at the end of December. They made quite an impression, but not necessarily a good one. In fact, the ferocity of the Canadian game frightened some Americans. The *New York Times* commented, "If we played this game in our colleges, it would be stopped by the police within one month as too great a menace to life. It is a good enough game when played slowly and phlegmatically, but it would never be safe to permit our college men to indulge in it."

The members of the 1909 team were richly rewarded by the standards of the time: each player was given a sweater coat and his choice of a gold watch or diamond ring to the value of $100. So the entire team returned with enthusiasm for the 1910 season. But a problem arose that year, emanating from the federal government. A new Civil Service Act decreed that all government employees must stay on the job until 5:00 p.m., one hour longer than previously dictated, which created a problem in getting to practices for the many Ottawa players working in the public service.

The Rough Riders were involved in a controversy in 1912, following a disputed victory over Toronto. The enraged Varsity crowd stormed the field in a bloody-minded mood. They attacked Ottawa players and demanded the head of referee Billy McMartin, shrieking that he had sold them out. McMartin escaped by donning an Ottawa sweater and running with the players. Holed up in his Montreal house the following day, McMartin told an interviewer, "I had to disguise myself like a thief or murderer. They stoned the Ottawa players and followed us. I got half a brick on the head which caused a lump as big as a chicken's egg."

But their greatest risk oftimes came from within. Like their counterparts on Parliament Hill, Ottawa football could fracture along the most unimaginable fault lines. Former CFL quarterback Frank Cosentino, in his 1969 book *Canadian Football: The Grey Cup Years*, relates a religious schism that split the team: "In 1923 . . . the team was destroyed from within by a religious duel. According to Brian Timmis in an interview with the author, 'It reached the point where the Catholic linemen wouldn't open a hole for the Protestant backfielders and the Protestants wouldn't open them for the Catholics. Even on the sidelines, all the Catholics had to sit on a green bench and the Protestants on another.' "

By 1925, enough unity had been restored for the Senators to win their first Grey Cup by defeating the Winnipeg Tammany Tigers 24-1, then successfully defend the Cup the next year, downing the Unversity of Toronto 10-7. The 1925 game was played on an Ottawa field that was in disgraceful shape for a national final. Lansdowne Park wasn't fully upgraded until 1948, when the playing surface was totally rebuilt. A newspaper report noted, "The playing field was redug to a depth of 18 inches and given a new tile bottom, then it was crowned for proper drainage. Cars are not allowed to park on the far side of the field anymore, thus eliminating the hazard of having some player come out of the mess with a 1948 license plate imprinted on his kisser."

From the 1930s to mid-century, Ottawa challenged intermittently for the Cup, winning a unique two-game series against Balmy Beach in 1940, and, under coach Clem Crowe, witnessing the implosion of the Glenn Dobbs legend in 1951. Then they plunged into feckless torpor for a decade, until reawakening under the charge of "the Professor."

When Frank Clair came to Canada, he had never seen Canadian football. When he left, Canada had never seen anything like Frank Clair. From his green start in Toronto in 1950, the tall, cerebral, insecure man from Ohio created a coaching record in the CFL that is never likely to be bettered, particularly in the modern era where coaching tenure seldom exceeds six years.

Clair coached for nineteen CFL years. His teams made the playoffs seventeen times, including fourteen years in a row, won twenty-two playoff games and played in six Grey Cup finals. Those are all records.

His five Grey Cup victories is a record tied only by Hugh Campbell, who had a run of five straight with the Eskimos from 1978 through 1982. Clair's all-time record in regular season games was 147 victories, 106 losses, 7 ties. Playoff record, 22-17-1. Grey Cup, 5-1. Overall, 174-124-8. Not too shabby for a guy who didn't know a rouge from a radish when he came north.

Canada had never seen

anything like Frank Clair.

Clair was the very antithesis of the coaching cliché: the thick-muscled, monosyllabic football general with the military haircut and matching persona. Clair wore raincoats and dark suits and snap-brim fedoras on the sidelines during games. His eyes, behind heavy horn-rimmed glasses, always had a slightly remote cast. He stood on the edge of the field, tall, beleaguered but noble, like Gary Cooper in *High Noon*. This combination of traits led logically to his nickname, "the Professor," but at times "the Absent-Minded Professor" might have been more accurate.

There are lovely anecdotes about Clair's apparent lapses in reality, like the time he threw his clipboard down on the ground, walked a dozen paces up the sideline, returned, looked down and asked the bench who had thrown his clipboard in the mud. About Clair's inability to remember his players' names. About his meanderings in time and space: Eddie McCabe recalls talking to Clair on the telephone; Clair, after putting a cigarette in his mouth, asked McCabe, "Eddie, have you got a match?" In one story, Clair discusses draft choices with his staff: "I think we should get this kid Paul Abraham." Assistant: "Coach, his name is Paul Moses." Clair: "Yeah, the guy from the Bible."

But absent-minded men do not win football championships; totally absorbed men do. That was Clair's special talent and his curse: at all times, he was immersed in the football problem of the moment. It made him a winner and it made him a worrier. He suffered from ulcers, sleeplessness, stress, insecurity, heart problems and back spasms.

Russ Jackson today recalls Clair's singularity of focus: "I had a great relationship with him because I understood him. I knew about his famous absent-mindedness, but that applied outside of football. In football, he was single-minded, had a great football mind and was a great innovator."

Weekend Magazine writer Bob McKeown, in a 1969 profile of Clair entitled "Worrying Is a Way of Life for Frank Clair," wrote, "It has been said that Frank Clair dies a little each game day. This is an understatement. Clair practically expires at the opening whistle and his condition deteriorates rapidly until his [Rough Riders] have the game won.

"Clair on the sidelines is at once tense and pensive. Immaculately dressed in good weather, he paces up and down or stands with hands on hips, his face reflecting all the emotions from gloom to doom."

Clair's wife, Pat, said, "After all, his whole job depends on 14 games which last just two hours each. I naturally worry when he loses."

He seldom raised his voice, but when he did the effect was startling. On one occasion, after a severe loss to Montreal, Clair heard his players snickering on the bus. He stopped the bus, unloaded the team and informed them that he did not wish to be associated with players who could laugh after a loss and that those who did should seek immediate work elsewhere. Another time, following a return flight from Vancouver, where his team had trashed some hotel rooms and then become drunkenly disruptive on the airplane, he assembled the team outside the airport and tore a creative strip off them. There was a stunned silence, broken only by a tinkling crash as a player dropped his pint from shaking fingers.

Clair had won Grey Cups with Toronto in 1950 and 1952. His future with the Argos must have looked as rosy as an English garden at that point. But the Argos self-destructed, disrupted by the meddlesome presence of Harry Sonshine. Out of patience with Sonshine's interference, his ulcers raging, Clair quit his $12,000 Argo job and went to the University of Cincinnati at $5,000 and a few migraines less. Clair arrived in Ottawa in 1956 after the Rough Riders dismissed Chan Caldwell, who had replaced Clem Crowe. He set out on a four-year rebuilding job, replacing old bricks and rotting timbers.

At that time Russ Jackson was a sophomore at McMaster University. At Hamilton's Westdale High School, he had developed into the greatest schoolboy athlete the city had ever seen, in football, basketball and baseball. Jackson recalls, "My first involvement with organized sports was baseball, with the police-run minor leagues when I was ten or eleven. Basketball was number two. Football was number three because I didn't play it all until high school. Then came hockey, which I played a little bit.

"My first aspiration of being a professional athlete was in baseball. When I was about fifteen, I was scouted by the New York Yankees and taken to a ten-day tryout camp in Oleana, New York. The problem was they wanted me to quit high school and sign with them and I wasn't about to do that.

"I was a third baseman and catcher. I guess the desire to be a catcher ties in with me wanting to be a quarterback. They are both positions where you are involved in every play, where every play is out in front of you and where you are in control." Although he played only two years of high school football—his mother told him he was too small—Jackson was Westdale's starting quarterback from the beginning.

By the time he had completed his five years at Westdale, Jackson was eighteen years old, an honours student, and he had grown up physically to six feet and 185 pounds of hard muscle and bone. Canadian college recruiters saw him and salivated like Pavlovian dogs. Four of them recruited him, McGill, Western, University of Toronto and Queen's, offering him what limited athletic scholarship aid was available. Jackson chose the one school that wanted his brain as much as his body, McMaster.

Al Smith, the McMaster football coach at the time, had visited Jackson and his parents and sold them on the school's great academic heritage. Jackson told biographer Eddie McCabe, "He convinced me that they had an athletic program I would be interested in, and their maths and physics program, in which I wanted to major, was second to none. They had the nuclear reactor right there on campus and any post-graduate work I wanted to do could certainly be done right there." And there was the practical aspect: "I didn't have any money and my folks weren't well off. McMaster was at home. I didn't want to leave college $5,000 or $10,000 in debt."

So Russ Jackson, super-jock, attended college on academic scholarships, becoming the classic Greek scholar-athlete. His ability to continue his studies depended on the results of his last calculus exam, not on how many touchdown passes he had pitched the previous Saturday. He flunked only one exam in his entire time at McMaster. His physics professor wrote on the failing paper, "Too much sport . . . not enough work."

It ate at Jackson's conscience like a cancer, and he vowed it would never happen again. And it didn't. He performed so brilliantly as a scholar that, in his final year, he was given a chance to become a Rhodes scholar, to do post-grad work at Oxford or Cambridge. After much soul-seaching, Jackson turned the opportunity down. He had decided he wanted to play professional football, saying in his biography, "Every waking hour since I was maybe six or seven years old had been spent throwing a baseball or a football, or playing hockey or doing something with athletics."

From the first scrimmage on his first day on the McMaster football team, Jackson was the starting quarterback. Coach Al Smith would remember, "He had the voice, the manner—even as a youngster at Westdale—of leadership. He seemed to be saying, 'I'm the leader, and don't dispute it.' He seems to have that feeling that he is not competing for a position. The position is his. You are competing for it."

One of the defining moments of Jackson's career occurred in his second year. McMaster was playing the Royal Military College of Kingston. Jackson ran the opening kickoff back for a touchdown, part of 30 points he scored on the day. RMC coach Tony Golab, a former Rough Rider star, told the pro club's general manager, Jim McCaffery, to remember Jackson's name and to make him a first choice in the Canadian college draft. McCaffery did just that, although there were dissenters. Hamilton's usually shrewd Jake Gaudaur passed on Jackson, as did the B.C. Lions' Herb Capozzi.

Even as a youngster, Jackson had the voice and the manners of a leader.

But there was a skeptic in Ottawa. It was Frank Clair. Clair and Jackson met for the first time over lunch in Toronto, where Jackson laid out what he wanted, and his demands were steep for Canadian rookies in the late 1950s. He wanted $5,000 to sign, $4,000 for his first year. Clair gulped but didn't quibble. He was not convinced that Jackson could play quarterback in the pros, but he was prepared to pay a premium price for a good halfback who could also play defence.

The legend has evolved that Jackson came to training camp in 1958 like a young Arthur, plucked Excalibur from the stone and was immediately crowned boy king of the quarterbacks. The fact is that he came to training camp as low man on the quarterback list, and it took him five years to get to the top. Clair had two veteran quarterbacks with pro experience, Tom Dimitroff, a pure thrower, and Hal Ledyard, a good enough passer and a magical ball-handler. Jackson would take a few snaps after those two had their fill. Then he would practice with the defence.

That's how it went through training camp, exhibition games and the season: Dimitroff and Ledyard were competing for the job, alternating as starters. Jackson was a defensive back who came in to mop up. He ran a limited series of option plays identical to the McMaster offence; he knew it, he excelled in it, he looked good in it, and he made a deeper impression on Ottawa spectators than he did on Clair.

Dimitroff was out by the seventh game with a broken leg, and Ledyard had the job. Ottawa finished third that year, upset Montreal in a sudden-death semi-final (Jackson ran in a pair of touchdowns) but were massacred by Hamilton in the two-game final. After that one, Clair said he was bringing in a new import quarterback the following season, and he did; he acquired Frank Tripucka, an immobile, dropback passer from Saskatchewan. He also brought Don Allard from Boston College and Babe Parilli from Green Bay.

And then there was the little guy from Wittenberg College in Ohio, a kid with a gun in his arm named Ron Lancaster. The rivalry between Lancaster and Jackson split the city of Ottawa in half as no political debate had ever done. There were times when Frank Clair was hesitant to go downtown for dinner, for fear of the hollering-at he would get about who should be quarterbacking the Riders. Jackson remembers, "In Ron's rookie year, he was in the position I had been in, backup quarterback trying to get a job as a defensive back. Then about the sixth or seventh game of the season, I fell on the ball and injured my ribcage and missed the only game of my career. Ronnie started that one and the whole thing started again. Sometimes we wouldn't know until game time who was going to start. It was a very tense situation for everyone, and it started to wear on Ronnie and me. We were both young kids and the indecision got to us. We found it really hard to prepare for the games with that uncertainty." The rivalry even increased the crowd hostility against Jackson; a bit of it had always been there, but Lancaster supporters cranked up the volume, despite the obvious improvements in Jackson's skills. He had learned ball-handling techniques from Ledyard and Tripucka, who had graciously spent hours with him, teaching him the mental side of passing.

Finally, Clair had to stop sidestepping on the quarterback issue and take a firm step forward, which he did in the summer of 1963 when, with some misgivings, he sold Lancaster to the Saskatchewan Roughriders. A rider attached to the sale gave Ottawa first rights of refusal on Lancaster's future services. It turned out to be a deal cut in heaven for both teams and for two future Hall of Fame quarterbacks. Says Jackson, "It had grown very uncomfortable for everyone—the coaches, the players, the fans and the media—and Frank [Clair] had to make a decision. So Ronnie went to Saskatchewan and I stayed. The great part of the story is that we both went on to have great careers. Think about how different it would have been for the league if one of us had been cut and sent home."

Meanwhile, Clair was developing a powerhouse team at the other positions. Two Canadians were key ingredients. Ron Stewart, a stumpy halfback who had scored more than 30 touchdowns during his university career at Queen's, had a continuing football problem: finding uniform pants small enough to fit his short legs. But once dressed, he was spectacular, a blistering runner, a dependable receiver and, despite standing only five-eight, a determined pass blocker. In a 1960 game against Montreal, Stewart ran for a total of 287 yards and 4 touchdowns. The other Canadian was Whit Tucker, a tall, leggy wide receiver who had explosive speed off the line and the ability to run under and catch Jackson's deepest bombs.

Bob Simpson, the veteran pass-catcher, was reaching the end of a great career but was a vital link in the passing game. Fullback Dave Thelen barely survived his first Rider training camp but hung on to become Mr. Inside to Stewart's Mr. Outside. Extremely shortsighted, Thelen wore contact lenses. A reporter asked Clair what Thelen did if his contacts became spattered with mud. "Then," replied Clair, "he plays strictly by Braille."

Under defensive coach Bill Smyth, the Riders had always, over the years, had ferocious linemen, blasters like Sam Scoccia, Kaye Vaughan, Bruno Bitkowski, Hardiman Cureton, Gilles Archambeault, Milt

Graham, Billy-Joe Booth (who Dick Beddoes once called "the best bald fat man playing defensive end in Canada") and Jim Conroy, and small but aggressive defensive backs like George Brancato, Gary Schreider, Joe Poirier, Bob O'Billovich and Davey West.

Ottawa players delighted in relating stories about Smyth, the bellowing ex-Marine. Clair usually left the pre-game speeches to Smyth, and they were pungent. Smyth would say, approximately, "Those ——s we're playing today are a bunch of thievin', lying ——s. Give them half a —— chance and they'll take the —— food out of your kids' mouths. So don't show them any —— mercy. Kick 'em in the ——s and knock them on their ——s. Now let's pray."

In the 1960 Grey Cup game against Edmonton, Clair alternated Jackson and Lancaster. The big play in the Riders' 16-6 victory was Lancaster's sleeper pass to Bill Sowalski, the last time the musty piece of trickery would be allowed in the CFL. But the victory was a tribute to Ottawa's defensive team. They held the Eskimos to 49 yards on the ground. Johnny Bright gained just 15 yards, Normie Kwong 7, and Jackie Parker was blanked on the ground. Ottawa rushed for 247 yards.

In the 1966 final, it was Roughrider against Rough Rider, Lancaster against Jackson. Jackson hit Tucker with two long touchdown passes, but Saskatchewan won it 29-14, largely due to George Reed's relentless bursts through the Ottawa line for 137 total yards.

In 1968, Jackson engineered a fourth-quarter comeback that led Ottawa to a 24-21 Grey Cup victory over Calgary. Trailing the Stampeders 14-11 at the end of the third quarter, the Rough Riders blew the game wide open on two plays. On one, running back Vic Washington took a pitchout from Jackson, fumbled the ball but regained it on a lucky bounce, then scooted 80 yards for a touchdown. On the other, ultra-speedy receiver Margene Adkins flew deep past Calgary defensive back Jerry Keeling and cradled a long pass from Jackson for a 70-yard score.

Then it was 1969, swan song time.

Ottawa finished first in the East at 11-3, Toronto second at 10-4. The Argos beat Hamilton in the semi-final and, after beating Ottawa 22-14 in the first game of the final, Toronto coach Leo Cahill challenged divine retribution by announcing that it would take "an act of God" to beat

Toronto. It didn't. It just took a 32-2 Ottawa victory in the second game to send the Rough Riders to the Grey Cup against Saskatchewan, the Argos home and Cahill in search of alternative worship.

On November 30 in Montreal's Autostade, thirty-three years old and greying at the temples, Russell Stanley Jackson gave Canada and Pierre Trudeau, who performed the ceremonial kickoff, something to remember.

Saskatchewan took a 9-0 lead on Lancaster's scoring pass to Al Ford, and a safety. Jackson took over and sang his aria. He threw a touchdown pass to Jay Roberts. Then, staring down the barrels of a full blitz, he hung on and threw an outlet pass to Stewart. The little halfback from Queen's, now a thirty-two-year-old veteran, ran it in 80 yards.

It was 14-9 Ottawa at the half. The green Riders kicked two singles in the third quarter, but then Jackson performed another miracle. Again running out of a collapsing pocket, on the 12, Jackson jittered and ducked under two tackles and was falling backwards when he threw on a line to Jim Mankins in the end zone.

There was more. In the fourth quarter, Saskatchewan's line pinned its collective ears back and chased Jackson out of the pocket. Later, Saskatchewan linebacker Cliff Shaw would say, "He had the ball when I hit him. I couldn't figure out why he didn't have it when we hit the ground." That's because Jackson, off balance, falling, had forced the ball to Stewart, who took it 32 yards for the another improvised touchdown. In the 29-11 Ottawa victory, Jackson had thrown 4 touchdown passes and held the ball on the converts, having a hand in all his team's points.

How do you top that? You don't. You walk away from it. The day after the game, Jackson announced his retirement. In 1960, Dick Beddoes had written, "Canadian quarterbacks aren't extinct like the great auk, but they ain't very tinct either." When Russ Jackson hung up his gear for the last time, Canadian quarterbacks in the Canadian Football League took an insecure perch on the endangered species list.

Jackson had played his entire career in Ottawa, the nation's capital, the seat of government, a place of intense media scrutiny. He was the all-Canadian boy, an all-star year after year, carrying an enormous weight of expectation. Was it tough to be Russ Jackson? "Not as much as some people have speculated," he says today. "We were the only professional team in town. Players were looked up to, and we respected that. It might have been tougher in a bigger city, like Toronto or Montreal, where demands are higher. But really, it was a neat thing. The attention we got was quite different from the political aspect of Ottawa, and I think all our players enjoyed the notoriety. For all twelve seasons I played, I had my home phone number listed in the book, and I never received a single angry call.

"Remember, all the time I was playing football, I was also teaching school. I used to say that 1,500 students and 3,000 parents had a piece of Russ Jackson, and it created its own form of respect on both sides."

Ten days later after Jackson retired, Frank Clair announced he was quitting coaching and taking over as general manager of the Rough Riders. Twenty days after the great victory, the Grey Cup was stolen from the Lansdowne Park trophy room. It was found fifty-nine days later in a hotel locker in Toronto.

There is an epilogue to the saga of Jackson and Clair, and it is not a happy one.

When Jackson retired, Clair said he felt Jackson had another ten playing years. Hamilton general manager Ralph Sazio said Jackson could stay on top for three more years. The B.C. Lions offered him $100,000 to play quarterback and complete his master's degree at U.B.C. Generously, the Ottawa *Citizen*'s editorial page endorsed the move, conceding that a CFL with Jackson in an enemy uniform would be better than a CFL with no Jackson at all. But Jackson got his $100,000 from an unlikely source. He heard the siren song and signed a five-year contract to coach the Toronto Argos starting in 1975. It was the first grievously bad decision he had ever made. He didn't have a minute of coaching experience in his career portfolio, and he was faced with a new, self-centred type of football player. He lasted two miserable seasons. He feuded with players, one of whom said that Jackson's game plan could be written on the head of a pin. Jackson was fired twelve days after a 6-7-1 second season. If the firing hurt, so too did Argo owner Bill Hodgson's second-thought statement in 1978 that he might have been too hasty in firing Jackson.

As for Clair, he might have been too sensitive, too naive a man to be a general manager. As superior as he was on the sidelines, battling other coaches, he became a victim in the front office, where the dollar was the bottom line. In December 1969, he signed a four-year contract to manage the Rough Riders, with his assistant, Jack Gotta, succeeding him as head coach. "The new job is a great challenge," Clair told reporters at the time. But he was giving up too much power. Gotta would have the final say on hirings, firings and trades.

With Clair in the front office, the Riders won two more Grey Cups, in 1973 (after winning nine of their last ten games) and the 1976 Roughrider-Rough Rider rematch. That was a jewel of a game, decided 23-20 on Tony Gabriel's dramatic catch of a Tom Clements pass with twenty seconds on the clock. The crowd of 53,467 generated the CFL's first million-dollar gate. Every point in the game was scored by Canadian players.

Clair was turfed as general manager in the off-season of 1978, victim of a series of ownership changes. He was replaced by former team president Jake Dunlap who, ironically, had been one of the first Argonaut players Clair had disciplined when he arrived in Toronto. Clair was kept on through a series of humiliating demotions. In 1980, he was fired again as director of personnel, and in 1982 he was hired as a roving scout by the Argonauts. This time Clair let his feelings hang out, saying he was relieved to be free of the boardroom turmoil in Ottawa. His bitterness was palpable when he said, "In Ottawa it was a case of Jake Dunlap shoving me out and him taking over when he really never had much knowledge of football. I feel I was treated unjustly. I just couldn't work with Dunlap. He and I never saw eye to eye."

There was something of a reconciliation in 1987. The Ottawa stadium was renamed Frank Clair Stadium and Clair, just before his seventieth birthday, was brought back as a part-time Ottawa scout for the U.S. small colleges.

Never before and never again in Canadian football would a coach and a quarterback ride so far and so long together. If we think of it that way, as a highway journey across Canada, we must think of Jackson insisting on being the driver, with the fretful Clair in the passenger seat, warning Jackson to avoid the pothole, to slow down, to steer with both hands.

In the end, they drove too far. They ran out of gas and a wheel fell off.

But what a ride it had been. And perhaps the going up was worth the coming down.

Overtime

The game has just ended. The field and the grandstand seats are empty as the spectators pick their way through the parking lot, marvelling at the hellacious lick the linebacker laid on that running back on the final drive of the game.

In the dressing room, players are peeling off layers of sweat-sodden sweaters and tape, like snakes shedding skin. The losers look at their feet and curse quietly. The winners earnestly tell how they did it, speaking into the banks of television lights and reporters' microphones that weave in front of their faces like strike-poised cobras. At one time in the history of this game, their words would have been written down with stubby pencils onto folded copy paper. But this is the electronic age.

By himself for a few minutes, the losing coach holds his head in his hands, trying to fathom how such a carefully plotted game plan could have gone so completely, so horribly, wrong. The winning coach shows the world a smile of certitude while inside he rejoices that his kids can probably finish the year at the same school.

Upstairs in the press room, serious young reporters coax the game details onto the flickering screens of their laptops. Nearby, in the press lounge, Annis Stukus and Jim Coleman, who have seen it all, are insisting that pencil and paper were better. Coleman will add that the best football was the football when teams travelled by train. Stukus will conclude an argument with the thunderous declaration, "But I invented the bloody game!"

Another night of Canadian football is ending. They will do it all again in another week through another Canadian winter, this game that is older than anyone who might be reading these words. It began in another century, has endured this twentieth, and seems certain to fascinate us as we pass the year 2000. It is our game, more so than the hockey that has been taken away from us, and is dominated by, the Americans—who, having swiped the Grey Cup once in 1995, have since been blessedly repulsed.

Canadian football, our football, is part of our culture, as rigidly fixed in our psyches as the notion that, if you do it right, you can get it done in three downs. We look at the old pictures and we see husky young Canadian men playing the game bare-headed. We see the transition to leather helmets and then to high-tech headgear with protective cages that could house parrots. And we do not care to think too long about modern players who put on gold jewellery to prepare for combat.

The game endures but changes. The geography made some radical shifts in the middle 1990s, as football was marketed to American cities where they wouldn't know an Ab Box if they uncrated one or appreciate a Red Storey if they heard one. But now the league has retreated back north of the border, where we know it should be.

The faces surely change. Players come and go and have the shelf-life of bruised veal. The coaches surely change. A wise old Winnipeg Blue Bomber coach named Reg Threlfall said in 1937, "Coaching a football team is a high-risk profession. Just when you think you're doing okay, some son-of-a-bitch saunters across the field and pokes a sharp stick in your eye."

In the idleness of the off-seasons, we take out our thrills and fondle them. Parker's run, Faloney's runback, Sam's arm, Wayne Harris's linebacking at 190 pounds. We will recall Terry Evanshen's balletic pass-catching and feel a pang; since a terrible automobile accident wiped out his long-term memory, Evanshen cannot remember his great plays.

We envy them their greatness, all those who played the Canadian game, and we who have only watched can only dimly fathom the poignance of some parting words by Calgary's great defender John Helton. He played fourteen seasons, played in two Grey Cup games. But he told Vancouver *Sun* columnist Archie McDonald of his empty feelings an hour after winning the 1971 Grey Cup game in Vancouver. "We went back across the bridge to the Coach House where the people were having a crazy time. We looked at each other and said, 'Is this all there is?' I don't know what we expected. Maybe we were let down because it was the end of the season. But it was a bit like being Cinderella coming home at five minutes after twelve."

One by one the lights flicker out around the rim of the grandstand. They'll come on again for next week's game. They always do.

Just the Facts

Shown on these pages are selected statistics from the postwar quarter-century. Statistics in the early years of this era were kept erratically if they were kept at all. When making comparisons, it must be remembered that length of season and number of playoff games increased over this period. Career statistics are given for complete CFL careers, even though some stray well into the 1970s; a player ought not to be punished for longevity. The following statistics are based on those found in *Canadian Football League: Facts, Figures and Records*, an annual publication of the CFL (and they are available on the CFL website at www.cfl.ca.).

Top 10 Career Touchdowns

TD	Player	Years
137	George Reed (Sas)	1963–75
91	Dick Shatto (Tor)	1954–65
88	Jackie Parker (Edm-Tor-BC)	1954–68
86	Willie Fleming (BC)	1959–68
83	Normie Kwong (Cal-Edm)	1948–60
80	Terry Evanshen (Mon-Cal-Ham-Tor)	1965–78
79	Virgil Wagner (Mon)	1946–54
"	Leo Lewis (Win)	1955–66
"	Hal Patterson (Mon-Ham)	1954–67
71	Johnny Bright (Cal-Edm)	1952–64

Top 5 Career Rushing

Player	Yds	Avg
George Reed (Sas)	16116	5.0
Johnny Bright (Cal-Edm)	10909	5.5
Normie Kwong (Cal-Edm)	9022	5.2
Leo Lewis (Win)	8861	6.5
Dave Thelen (Ott-Tor)	8463	5.5

Top 5 Career Average Gain Pass Receiving *(200 or more passes)*

Player	Avg	Catches	Yds	Years
Whit Tucker (Ott)	22.4	272	6092	1962–70
Bob Simpson (Ott)	22.0	274	6034	1954–62
Hal Patterson (Mon-Ham)	20.6	460	9473	1954–67
Tommy Grant (Ham-Win)	19.9	329	6542	1956–69
Jim Thorpe (Tor-Win)	19.6	209	4091	1969–72

Top 5 Career Passers *(ranked by completion percentage, minimum 2500 attempts)*

Player	Att	Comp	%	Yds	Avg	Int	TD
Sam Etcheverry (Mon)	2829	1630	.7.6	25582	15.7	166	183
Peter Liske (Tor-Cal-BC)	2571	1441	56.4	21266	14.7	133	130
Joe Kapp (Cal-BC)	2709	1406	54.5	22725	15.4	130	136
Ron Lancaster (Ott-Sas)	6233	3384	54.3	50535	14.9	396	333
Russ Jackson (Ott)	2530	1356	53.6	24592	18.1	125	185

Top 5 Career Pass Interceptions

INT	Player	Years
59	Garney Henley (Ham)	1960–75
58	Don Sutherin (Ham-Ott-Tor)	1958–70
52	John Wydareny (Tor-Edm)	1963–72
51	Ed Learn (Mon-Tor)	1958–69
50	Larry Robinson (Cal)	1961–74

Leading Rushers, 1950–70

	West	Yds	East	Yds
1950	Tom Casey (Win)	637	n/a	
1951	Normie Kwong (Edm)	933	n/a	
1952	Johnny Bright (Cal)	815	n/a	
1953	Billy Vessels (Edm)	926	n/a	
1954	Howard Waugh (Cal)	1043	Alex Webster (Mon)	984
1955	Normie Kwong (Edm)	1250	Pat Abbruzzi (Mon)	1248
1956	Normie Kwong (Edm)	1437	Pat Abbruzzi (Mon)	1062
1957	Johnny Bright (Edm)	1679	Gerry McDougall (Ham)	1053
1958	Johnny Bright (Edm)	1722	Gerry McDougall (Ham)	1109
1959	Johnny Bright (Edm)	1340	Dave Thelen (Ott)	1339
1960	Earl Lunsford (Cal)	1343	Dave Thelen (Ott)	1407
1961	Earl Lunsford (Cal)	1794	Don Clark (Mon)	1143
1962	Nub Beamer (BC)	1161	George Dixon (Mon)	1520
1963	Lovell Coleman (Cal)	1343	George Dixon (Mon)	1270
1964	Lovell Coleman (Cal)	1629	Ron Stewart (Ott)	867
1965	George Reed (Sas)	1768	Dave Thelen (Ott)	801
1966	George Reed (Sas)	1409	Don Lisbon (Mon)	1007
1967	George Reed (Sas)	1471	Bo Scott (Ott)	762
1968	George Reed (Sas)	1222	Bill Symons (Tor)	1107
1969	George Reed (Sas)	1353	Dennis Duncan (Mon)	1037
1970	Hugh McKinnis (Cal)	1135	Bill Symons (Tor)	908

Leading Pass Receivers, 1950-70

	West	No.	East	No.
1950	Morris Bailey (Edm)	67	n/a	
1951	Bob Shaw (Cal)	61	n/a	
1952	Paul Salata (Cal)	65	n/a	
1953	Bud Grant (Win)	68	n/a	
1954	Bud Grant (Win)	49	Al Pfeifer (Tor)	68
1955	Willie Roberts (Cal)	59	Red O'Quinn (Mon)	78
1956	Bud Grant (Win)	63	Hal Patterson (Mon)	88
1957	Jack Gotta (Cal)	39	Red O'Quinn (Mon)	61
1958	Jack Hill (Sas)	60	Red O'Quinn (Mon)	65
1959	Ernie Pitts (Win)	68	Red O'Quinn (Mon)	53
1960	Gene Filipski (Cal)	47	Dave Mann (Tor)	61
			Hal Patterson (Mon)	61
1961	Farrell Funston (Win)	47	Dave Mann (Tor)	53
1962	Tommy Joe Coffey (Edm)	65	Dick Shatto (Tor)	47
1963	Bobby Taylor (Cal)	74	Dick Shatto (Cal)	67
1964	Tommy Joe Coffey (Edm)	81	Dick Shatto (Tor)	53
1965	Tommy Joe Coffey (Edm)	81	Terry Evanshen (Mon)	37
1966	Terry Evanshen (Cal)	67	Bobby Taylor (Tor)	56
1967	Terry Evanshen (Cal)	96	Bobby Taylor (Tor)	53
1968	Ken Nielsen (Win)	68	Bobby Taylor (Tor)	56
1969	Herm Harrison (Cal)	68	Tommy Joe Coffey (Ham)	71
1970	Herm Harrison (Cal)	70	Dave Fleming (Ham)	56

Top 5 Winningest Coaches, 1950-70

Coach	Regular Season			Playoffs			Grey Cup		Overall		
	W	L	T	W	L	T	W	L	W	L	T
Frank Clair (Tor 50-54; Ott 56-59)	147	106	7	22	17	1	5	1	174	124	8
Bud Grant (Win 57-66)	102	56	2	16	9	1	4	2	122	67	3
Jim Trimble (Ham 56-62; Mon 63-65)	77	61	2	9	7	0	1	4	87	72	2
Douglas Walker (Mon 52-59)	59	48	1	6	6	0	0	3	65	57	1
Frank Ivy (Edm 54-57)	50	14	0	8	4	0	3	0	61	18	0

The Grey Cup, 1945–70

	Score	Winner	Loser	Location	Attendance
1945	35–0	Toronto	Winnipeg	Toronto	18,660
1946	28–6	Toronto	Winnipeg	Toronto	18,960
1947	10–9	Toronto	Winnipeg	Toronto	18,885
1948	12–7	Calgary	Ottawa	Toronto	20,013
1949	28–15	Montreal	Calgary	Toronto	20,087
1950	13–0	Toronto	Winnipeg	Toronto	27,101
1951	21–14	Ottawa	Saskatchewan	Toronto	27,341
1952	21–11	Toronto	Edmonton	Toronto	27,391
1953	12–6	Hamilton	Winnipeg	Toronto	27,313
1954	26–25	Edmonton	Montreal	Toronto	27,321
1955	34–19	Edmonton	Montreal	Vancouver	39,417
1956	50–27	Edmonton	Montreal	Toronto	27,425
1957	32–7	Hamilton	Winnipeg	Toronto	27,051
1958	35–28	Winnipeg	Hamilton	Vancouver	36,567
1959	21–7	Winnipeg	Hamilton	Toronto	33,133
1960	16–6	Ottawa	Edmonton	Vancouver	38,102
1961	21–14	Winnipeg	Hamilton	Toronto	32,651
1962	28–27	Winnipeg	Hamilton	Toronto	32,655
1963	21–10	Hamilton	B.C.	Vancouver	36,545
1964	34–24	B.C.	Hamilton	Toronto	32,655
1965	22–16	Hamilton	Winnipeg	Toronto	32,655
1966	29–14	Saskatchewan	Ottawa	Vancouver	36,553
1967	24–1	Hamilton	Saskatchewan	Ottawa	31,358
1968	24–21	Ottawa	Calgary	Toronto	32,655
1969	29–11	Ottawa	Saskatchewan	Montreal	33,172
1970	23–10	Montreal	Calgary	Toronto	32,669

Most Outstanding Player, 1953–70

1953	Billy Vessels (Edm)	1962	George Dixon (Mon)
1954	Sam Etcheverry (Mon)	1963	Russ Jackson (Ott)
1955	Pat Abbruzzi (Mon)	1964	Lovell Coleman (Cal)
1956	Hal Patterson (Mon)	1965	George Reed (Sas)
1957	Jackie Parker (Edm)	1966	Russ Jackson (Ott)
1958	Jackie Parker (Edm)	1967	Peter Liske (Cal)
1959	Johnny Bright (Edm)	1968	Bill Symons (Tor)
1960	Jackie Parker (Edm)	1969	Russ Jackson (Ott)
1961	Bernie Faloney (Ham)	1970	Ron Lancaster (Sas)

Most Outstanding Canadian, 1954-70

1954	Gerry James (Win)	1963	Russ Jackson (Ott)
1955	Normie Kwong (Edm)	1964	Tommy Grant (Ham)
1956	Normie Kwong (Edm)	1965	Zeno Karcz (Ham)
1957	Gerry James (Win)	1966	Russ Jackson (Ott)
1958	Ron Howell (Ham)	1967	Terry Evanshen (Cal)
1959	Russ Jackson (Ott)	1968	Ken Nielsen (Win)
1960	Ron Stewart (Ott)	1969	Russ Jackson (Ott)
1961	Tony Pajaczkowski (Cal)	1970	Jim Young (BC)
1962	Harvey Wylie (Cal)		

Most Outstanding Lineman, 1955-70

1955	Tex Coulter (Mon)	1963	Tom Brown (BC)
1956	Kaye Vaughan (Ott)	1964	Tom Brown (BC)
1957	Kaye Vaughan (Ott)	1965	Wayne Harris (Cal)
1958	Don Luzzi (Cal)	1966	Wayne Harris (Cal)
1959	Roger Nelson (Edm)	1967	Ed McQuarters (Sas)
1960	Herb Gray (Win)	1968	Ken Lehmann (Ott)
1961	Frank Rigney (Win)	1969	John Lagrone (Edm)
1962	John Barrow (Ham)	1970	Wayne Harris (Cal)

Best Efforts, 1945-70

Most TDs, One Season

20   Pat Abbruzzi (Mon)   1956

Most TDs, One Game

6   Bob McNamara (Win) [vs B.C., Oct 13, 1956]

Most Yards Rushing, One Season

1,794   Earl Lunsford (Cal)   1961

Most Yards Rushing, One Game

287   Ron Stewart (Ott) (15 carries) [vs Mon, Oct 10, 1960]

Most Yards Pass Receiving, One Season

1,914   Hal Patterson (Mon)   1956

Most Yards Pass Receiving, One Game

338   Hal Patterson (Mon) (11 catches) [vs Ham, Sept 29, 1956]

Most Yards Passing, One Game

586   Sam Etcheverry (Mon) [vs Ham, Oct 14, 1954]

Longest Field Goal (Yds)

59   Dave Cutler (Edm) [vs Sas, Oct 28, 1970]

Longest Interception Return (Yds)

120   Neal Beaumont (BC) [vs Sas, Oct 12, 1963]

Most Combined Yardage, One Game

381   Hal Patterson (Mon) [vs Ham, Sept 29, 1956]

Scoring Leaders, 1945-70

	West	Pts.	East	Pts.
1945	n/a		Royal Copeland (Tor)	40
1946	Bill Wusyk (Cal)	32	Joe Krol (Tor)	65
			Virgil Wagner (Mon)	65
1947	Gabe Patterson (Sas)	36	Virgil Wagner (Mon)	71
1948	Paul Rowe (Cal)	35	Virgil Wagner (Mon)	60
1949	Vern Graham (Cal)	58	Virgil Wagner (Mon)	77
1950	Joe Aguirre (Win)	57	Edgar Jones (Ham)	108
1951	Bob Shaw (Cal)	61	John Logan (Ham)	51
1952	Bob Shaw (Cal)	110	Ulysses Curtis (Tor)	80
1953	Bud Korchak (Win)	66	Gene Roberts (Ott)	88
1954	Joe Aguirre (Sas)	85	Alex Webster (Mon)	80
1955	Ken Carpenter (Sas)	90	Al Pfeifer (Tor)	98
1956	Buddy Leake (Win)	103	Pat Abbruzzi (Mon)	120
1957	Gerry James (Win)	131	Hal Patterson (Mon)	78
1958	Jack Hill (Sas)	145	Bill Bewley (Mon)	62
1959	Jackie Parker (Edm)	109	Cookie Gilchrist (Tor)	75
1960	Gerry James (Win)	114	Cookie Gilchrist (Tor)	115
1961	Jackie Parker (Edm)	104	Don Sutherin (Ham)	69
1962	Tommy Joe Coffey (Edm)	129	George Dixon (Mon)	90
1963	George Fleming (Win)	135	Dick Shatto (Tor)	81
1964	Larry Robinson (Cal)	106	Don Sutherin (Ham)	94
1965	Larry Robinson (Cal)	95	Don Sutherin (Ham)	82
1966	Hugh Campbell (Sas)	102	Moe Racine (Ott)	71
1967	Terry Evanshen (Cal)	102	Tommy Joe Coffey (Ham)	107
1968	Ted Gerela (BC)	115	Don Sutherin (Ham)	112
1969	Jack Abendschan (Sas)	116	Tommy Joe Coffey (Ham)	148
1970	Jack Abendschan (Sas)	116	Tommy Joe Coffey (Ham)	113

Sources and Acknowledgements

History in the context of Canadian football is more a matter of consensus than of incontrovertible record. Printed sources vary, memories are subjective, and statistical record-keeping has been at times haphazard. So we have been fortunate in writing this book to have benefited from the work of those who have gone before us.

First, we must thank those who shared with us their memories. Most notable among these are those who played or built the game, including Bob Ackles, Herb Capozzi, Bill Clancey, Jim Carphin, Sam Etcheverry, Bernie Faloney, Norm Fieldgate, Al Ford, Jake Gaudaur, Russ Jackson, Eagle Keys, Allan McEachern, Ken Ploen, Frank Rigney, Pete Thodos and especially the inimitable Annis Stukus. Just listing your names unleashes grand memories.

Then there were the scribes who witnessed that great era, including Laurie Artiss, Bryan Hall, Jim Kearney, Archie McDonald, Keith Matthews, Hal Sigurdson, Jim Taylor and the incomparable Jim Coleman. Their recollections were augmented by our scanning of several miles of microfilm of Canada's major daily newspapers from the postwar quarter- century. Our research of the printed record was also ably assisted by Shelley Fralic, Wayne Huizinga and the crack staff at the Pacific Press library. Our research on the visual side benefited greatly from the assistance of Janice Smith and her staff at the Canadian Football Hall of Fame, particularly Elizabeth Dagg, researcher extraordinaire.

Canadian football has been well served by a number of books. A close comparison of their texts generates an approximation of what actually happened. These include general works like Frank Cosentino's two volumes, *Canadian Football: The Grey Cup Years* (Musson, 1969) and *A Passing Game: A History of the CFL* (Bain & Cox, 1995); Gordon Currie, *100 Years of Canadian Football* (Pagurian, 1968); Jack Sullivan, *The Grey Cup Story* (Pagurian, 1974); Gordon Walker, *The Grey Cup Tradition* (ESP, 1987); Tony Allan, *Grey Cup Cavalcade* (Harlequin, 1959). There are books by analysts and observers: Jeffrey Goodman, *Huddling Up: The Inside Story of the CFL* (Fitzhenry & Whiteside, 1981); Jay Teitel, *The Argo Bounce*

(Lester & Orpen, Dennys, 1982); LaVerne Barnes, *The Plastic Orgasm* (McClelland & Stewart, 1971); Trent Frayne, *The Tales of an Athletic Supporter* (McClelland & Stewart, 1990). Then there is the insider's story: Leo Cahill with Scott Young, *Goodbye Argos* (McClelland & Stewart, 1973); Eddie McCabe, *Profile of a Pro: The Russ Jackson Story* (Prentice-Hall Canada, 1969); Dick Beddoes and Dave Skrien, *Countdown to Grey Cup* (McClelland & Stewart, 1965); Mel Profit, *For Love, Money and Future Considerations* (D.C. Heath, 1972); Jim Young with Jim Taylor, *Dirty 30* (Methuen, 1974). Some teams are well served by officially sanctioned histories, such as Jack Matheson, *60 Years and Running: Blue Bombers, 1930–1990* (Winnipeg Blue Bombers, 1990); Vince Leah, *A History of the Blue Bombers* (n.p., n.d.); Bob Calder and Garry Andrews, *Rider Pride: The Story of Canada's Best-Loved Football Team* (Western Producer, 1984); Merv Daub, *Gael Force: A Century of Football at Queen's* (McGill-Queen's University Press, 1996). In tracing the football story in the United States, the following were useful: Mickey Herskowitz, *The Golden Age of Pro Football: A Remembrance of Pro Football in the 1950s* (National Football League/Macmillan, 1974); Robert W. Peterson, *Pigskin: The Early Years of Pro Football* (Oxford University Press, 1997); David S. Neft and Richard M. Cohen, *The Football Encyclopedia: The Complete History of Pro Football from 1892 to the Present* (St. Martin's, 1991); Grantland Rice, *The Tumult and the Shouting: My Life in Sport* (A.S. Barnes, 1954). The Canadian Football League, the Canadian Football Hall of Fame and several teams have Internet websites with a historical component.

Lastly, we owe many thanks to Barbara Pulling of Greystone Books, an editor's editor, for smoothing out our disparate styles. We'll make a football fan of her yet.

Denny Boyd, West Vancouver
Brian Scrivener, Bowen Island
July 1997

Index

Chicowski, Chick, 30
Christian, Gord, 136
Clair, Frank "The Professor," 16, 17, 121, 143–44,
    147, 148, 149, 150, 152–53
Clancy, Bill, 11
Clancy, Tom "King," 141
Claridge, Bruce, 112
Claridge, Pat, 114
Clarke, Reg, 131
Clements, Tom, 153
Coffey, Tommy Joe, 84
Cohee, Dick, 134
Coleman, Jim, 9, 26, 45, 68, 79, 154, 155
Coleman, Lovell, 33–34
Conacher, Lionel "Big Train," 12–13, 16
Conroy, Jim, 150
Continental Football League, 21, 71
Copeland, Royal, 9, 10, 16
Cosentino, Frank, *Canadian Football: The Grey
    Cup Years*, 8, 143
Coulter, Bruce, 66
Coulter, Tex, 43, 58, 62, 64, 67, 68
Cradock, Eric, 59
Crane, Geoff, 78
Crawford, Bill, 112
Crowe, Clem, 110, 111, 112, 143, 145
Cunningham, Bob, 60
Cuozzo, Gary, 117
Cureton, Hardiman, 149
Currie, Gordon, *100 Years of Canadian Football*,
    26
Custis, Bernie, 84

Dalla Riva, Peter, 72
Dandurand, Leo, 59, 60–61
Dean, Bob, 45
Dekdebrun, Al, 16, 17
Delbridge, C. B. "Slim," 113, 114
DeMarco, Mario, 131–32
Dennis, Wayne "Whiskey," 95
Denson, Moses, 72
Desjardins, Pierre, 72
Dimitroff, Tom, 148
Dixon, George, 69
Dobbs, Glenn "The Dobber," 1, 21, 128, 129, 130,
    131, 143
Dobler, Wally, 10
Dojack, Paul, 51, 81
Dorais, Gus, 8, 9
Dorsch, Henry, 136
Druxman, George, 96
Dublinski, Tom, 18
Dumelie, Larry, 136
DuMoulin, Seppi, 74

Duncan, Dennis, 71
Duncan, Jim, 35, 136
Duncan, Randy, 112
Dunlap, Jake, 153
Dunn, Jimmy, 64
Dushinski, Ted, 136

Edmonton Eskimos, 7, 15, 17, 22, 26, 33, 34, 37–55,
    59, 60, 62, 64–66, 78–79, 80, 85, 91, 98, 107, 109,
    113, 120, 122, 125, 131, 150
Edwards, Danny, 110, 112
Elliot, Chaucer, 74
Esaw, Johnny, 99
Etcheverry, Sam "The Rifle," 4, 19, 39, 43, 44, 45,
    56–57, 58, 61–62, 63, 64, 65, 66, 68, 71, 72, 86,
    156
Ettinger, Donald "Red," 128, 129, 130
Evanshen, Terry, 35, 156
Evashevski, Forrest, 90
Eyre, Alan, 113

Faloney, Bernie, 42, 44, 50, 57–58, 59, 62, 64, 66,
    78–79, 80, 81, 84, 85–87, 156
Fears, Tommy, 63
Fieldgate, Norm, 48, 114, 118
Filchock, Frank, 30, 41, 59, 60, 61, 131, 132
Fleming, Willie, 83, 112, 114, 117, 118
Flutie, Doug, 22, 36
Fog Bowl. *See* Grey Cup, 1962
Ford, Allan, 123–24, 135, 136, 151
Fouts, Dick, 114
Frayne, Trent, 84, 125–26
Funston, Farrell, 34, 94, 95, 96, 99
Furlong, Jim, 72

Gabriel, Tony, 153
Galiffa, Arnie, 110, 111
Gaudaur, Jake, 57, 77, 78, 79, 81, 83, 84, 85, 147
George, Ed, 72
Getty, Don, 51, 52, 66, 78
Gilchrist, Cookie, 19, 79, 80, 81
Gillespie, Hec, 114
Gillman, Sid, 16
Glasser, Sully, 130
Golab, Tony, 147
Goldston, Ralph, 79, 91
Gotta, Jack, 153
Graham, Milt, 149
Grant, Harry Peter "Bud," 52, 80, 81, 82, 83,
    88–89, 90, 91, 92–93, 96–97, 100, 101, 102, 112
Grant, Tommy, 83
Gray, Herb, 96–97, 100
Grey Cup, 3, 5, 8, 10, 11, 16, 28, 29, 38, 53, 54, 55,
    56, 88, 98, 118, 133, 136, 139, 141, 143, 144, 152,